FAREWELL TO THE ASSIZES

FAREWELL TO THE ASSIZES

The Sixty-one Towns

by

BASIL NIELD

GARNSTONE PRESS
London

FAREWELL TO THE ASSIZES
is published for the author by
THE GARNSTONE PRESS LIMITED
59 Brompton Road, London SW3 1DS

ISBN: 0 85511 280 8

© Basil Nield, 1972

Printed and bound in Great Britain
by W & J Mackay Limited, Chatham

Author's Note

Having presided, during my years as a judge of the High Court, at each of the sixty-one assize towns in England and Wales, it was suggested that it might be of interest if I were to write something about these towns in particular and the assize system in general, especially in view of the proposal—now a decision—to abandon that system. This I have attempted to do. Let it be made clear—and none I think will doubt it—that this is my first effort in the field of letters, if such it can be called, and I well realize that I have no claim to literary prowess. None the less it is my hope that this work will interest and amuse some of those who read it.

It is important to notice that the substance of this work was written before the recommendations of the Commission presided over by Lord Beeching had been accepted—as they largely have been—and included in the Courts Act of 1971.

I have expressed my gratitude to various people for their help in my task in the course of the text and also in the list of acknowledgements. I would however like to mention some others who have given most generous aid. Among them are—

Several Lords Lieutenant of Counties.

Several High Sheriffs.

All the Under Sheriffs.

Many Town Clerks and Clerks of County Councils and Local Authority archivists.

Sir F. E. Pritchard and my sister, Miss Beryl Nield, who have read the proofs and made suggestions.

The Secretarial Services of Tunbridge Wells and Mrs. Deane of that organization for struggling with my recording tapes.

Mrs Edgar Harrad.

Mr Michael Balfour.

Mr Jamie Mackay Miller who has given me expert and kindly advice.

Miss Mary Anne Southby of Messrs W & J Mackay Limited.

My ex-clerk, Leonard Gullett, in the early stage.

My present clerk, Henry Milford, whose help has been invaluable.

Acknowledgements

It is desired to make grateful acknowledgement to the following, in addition to those who are mentioned in the text, for permission to quote from their works, to make use of information provided and to reproduce photographs:

Donald Baston, Esq., Birmingham Corporation, British Publishing Co. Ltd., Cardiff Corporation, Chelmsford Public Library, Borough of Devizes, Devon County Council, Borough of Dorset, Eagle Photos (Chelmsford) Ltd., D. Llewellyn Evans, Esq., Flintshire County Council, Borough of Haverfordwest, The Estate of Sir Alan Herbert, Hereford City Council and their Official Guide, Borough of Huntingdon & Godmanchester, City of Leicester Publicity Dept., Russell McClelland, Esq., G. W. May Ltd., W. F. Meadows, Esq., Melton & Rutland Journal, F. C. Merritt, Esq., Antony Miles Ltd., L. Morris, Esq., Nottingham City Engineer, Oakham Urban District Council, Pitkin Pictorials, County Borough of Reading, Borough of Shrewsbury, H. J. Smeeton, Esq., South Wales Evening Post, Dudley O. Spain, Esq., Borough of Warwick, Western Telegraph, J. Whitehead & Son (Appleby) Ltd, Wrayford Willmer, Esq., Winton Publications Ltd, Yorkshire Evening Press, Yorkshire Post Newspapers Ltd.

Contents

The Rt. Hon. Lord Widgery, P.C., O.B.E., T.D., Lord Chief Justice of England

Foreword

by

The Lord Chief Justice of England

To have sat as Judge of Assize at every one of the sixty-one former Assize towns of England and Wales is surely achievement enough, but such is the stuff of which Basil Nield is made that he can still write a most entertaining book about his experiences.

Those to whom the places and personalities are familiar will find this a fascinating and nostalgic reminder of circuit life in the sixties, and even the most avid collector of judicial anecdotes cannot fail to find something new for his repertoire.

Moreover, the book contains material for the serious historian who wishes to trace the development of the Assize system through its final stages.

Hodgen, C.J.

This book is for my sister Beryl
who suggested that I write it.

CHAPTER I

The Assizes

'ALL PERSONS having anything to do before my Lords the Queen's Justices of Assize of Oyer Terminer and General Gaol Delivery for this County draw near and give your attendance.

My Lords the Queen's Justices do strictly charge and command all persons to keep silence whilst Her Majesty's Commission of Assize is produced and read upon pain of imprisonment.'

'ELIZABETH THE SECOND by the Grace of God of the United Kingdom of Great Britain and Northern Ireland and of Our other Realms and Territories Queen Head of the Commonwealth Defender of the Faith to Our well beloved and faithful Counsellor the Lord High Chancellor of Great Britain

Our beloved and faithful Counsellor the Lord President of Our Council

Our most dear Cousin and Counsellor the Lord Keeper of Our Privy Seal

Our well beloved and faithful Counsellor the Lord Lieutenant of the County

Our well beloved and faithful Counsellor the Lord Chief Justice of England

Our Judges for the time being of Our Supreme Court of Judicature

such of Our Counsel learned in the Law as are for the time being authorized by Our Royal Warrant or by the Warrant of Our Lord High Chancellor to be of the Commission and the Clerk of Assize and Circuit Officers of the Circuit

GREETING KNOW YE that We have assigned you and any two of you of whom one of Our Judges of Our Supreme Court of Judicature or one of Our said Counsel learned in the Law shall be one OUR JUSTICES to enquire more fully the truth by the oath of good and lawful men of Our Counties of all offences and injuries whatsoever within our said Counties and to hear and determine the premises and to deliver the Gaols of Our said Counties of the Prisoners therein being and to take all the Assizes Juries and Certificates before whatsoever Justices arraigned within Our said Counties

AND THEREFORE WE COMMAND you that at certain days and places which you shall appoint for this purpose you and any two of you as aforesaid shall make diligent enquiries about the said injuries and offences and hear and determine the same within Our said Counties and deliver the Gaols of Our said Counties of the prisoners therein being and take all those Assizes Juries and Certificates within Our said Counties doing therein what to justice does appertain according to the laws and customs of England saving to Us the amerciaments and other things from thence to Us accruing AND WE COMMAND AND EMPOWER you to do in the execution of this Commission all things which have heretofore been lawfully done in obedience to Our Commissions of Oyer and Terminer General Gaol Delivery Assize and Association and Our Writs of Association and Si non omnes AND WE WILL that this Commission shall be deemed to be a Commission of Oyer and Terminer a Commission of General Gaol Delivery and a Commission of Assize.

IN WITNESS whereof We have caused these Our Letters to be made Patent WITNESS Ourself at Westminster'

'GOD SAVE THE QUEEN.

Mr High Sheriff of this County be pleased to produce the several writs and precepts to you directed and delivered and returnable here this day so that my Lords the Queen's Justices may proceed thereon.'

Thus traditionally for many generations the assizes have been opened in each of the sixty-one assize towns in England and Wales.

Originally the courts followed the person of the King and those seeking justice therefore had to undergo the expense, delay and frustration of pursuing the King in his constant movements about the countryside and even abroad. Indeed it is recorded that one plaintiff followed the King through England and France for five years before his case could be heard. All this was changed.

Section 17 of the Statute of 1215, Magna Carta, provided:

Common Pleas shall not follow our Court but shall be held in some certain place.

The certain place, although not named in the Charter, turned out to be Westminster and all writs of assize had to be dealt with there or await trial in the locality in which they had originated.

The justices itinerant were first appointed after the Assize of Clarendon in 1166 and in 1196 at the Council of Northampton, the Kingdom was divided into six areas for the purposes of the itinerant justices, there being then one to each area. To avoid delay and inconvenience Magna Carta further provided that certain trials might be heard by the justices in Eyre, that is to say judges of the High Court travelling to each county at least once a year. By successive enactments the civil jurisdiction of the justices of assize was extended and the number of their sittings was increased until the necessity for the litigant to travel to Westminster was almost obviated. An Act of Edward I provided that the writ summoning the jury to Westminster should also appoint a time and place for hearing the cases in the county of origin. The date of the summons to Westminster was always subsequent to the date for the hearing in the county and so timed to fall in the vacation preceding the Westminster term, and thus 'unless before' or Nisi Prius issues came to be dealt with by the justices of assize before the summons to Westminster could take effect. It is to be presumed that the form of summons to Westminster required the litigants attendance there, 'Nisi Prius', that is unless the suit is dealt with before in the place of origin.

It is to be noticed that Section 18 of Magna Carta provided

Land disputes shall be taken only in their proper Counties and in this manner: We, or if We be absent from the realm Our Chief Justiciary shall send two Justiciaries through each County four times a year and they together with four Knights elected out of each County by the people thereof, shall hold the said Assize in the County Court on the day and in the place where that Court meets.

The assize system has changed very little since mediaeval times and judges of the High Court, as everyone knows, still travel from London on circuit normally sitting in each county town.

At the end of 1960 an Inter-departmental Committee, under the chairmanship of Mr Justice Streatfeild, recommended that the itineraries of the judges and the order in which assize towns were to be visited, should be reorganized in a new scheme aimed principally at the more expeditious disposal of both criminal and civil assize work. It was this reorganized system which fell to be considered when, in May 1967, a Royal Commission under the chairmanship of Lord Beeching was set up 'to enquire into the present arrangements for the administration of justice at Assizes and at Quarter Sessions outside Greater London, and to report what reforms should be made for the more convenient economic and efficient disposal of the Civil and Criminal business at present dealt with by those Courts'.

The Report of the Royal Commission was presented to Parliament in September 1969. The Report's basic recommendations include

(i) that a new superior court of criminal justice be created to be called the Crown Court which shall absorb the criminal jurisdiction at present exercised by Courts of Assize and Quarter Sessions and some other Courts;

(ii) that the High Court shall have jurisdiction throughout England and Wales, to sit when and where needed;

(iii) that a new permanent bench of Circuit judges be established.

The Commission recommended that there should be six circuits (in this way proposing to follow the respectable precedent provided by the Council of Northampton in 1196) with administrative centres at Birmingham, Leeds, Manchester, London, Cardiff and Bristol.

Thus it will be seen that the assizes, as they have been known for so long, will cease to exist and there will be no need for a Royal Commission to authorize the attendance of judges of the High Court in the counties.

It is with these far-reaching changes in mind that I have thought that it might be of interest to make some record describing the Sixty-one Towns and the traditions and customs which are met with by a judge on circuit and I hope I shall be forgiven if some personal reminiscences under the 'old order' are included here.

Setting out from London, if the judge of assize goes by train, he is entitled to a reserved carriage. This is just one way of securing that there shall be no danger of the judge coming into contact with any litigant or juryman, or even accused on bail. The importance of this is illustrated by a true happening.

The judge's marshal—and a word as to his functions later—stood guard one day at the door of the reserved carriage at Paddington before his judge arrived to take the assize at Taunton. As the time drew near for the train to leave, a young man burst into the carriage saying 'I can't find a seat anywhere. Who is this carriage reserved for anyway?' The marshal advised him to read the reservation notice on the window. This he did and read 'Reserved for Judge of Assize'. The young officer gathered his bags and ran. At Taunton the next morning he was the first defendant in the criminal calendar and was put up in the dock charged with a serious driving offence.

Arrived at his destination the judge is met by the High Sheriff or the Under Sheriff of the county, formally attired. Very often the stationmaster is also there to meet him and escort him to the car provided by the High Sheriff. This is usually an elderly, black Rolls-Royce, hired from a local firm, and frequently engaged upon more melancholy excursions. The judge is conveyed to his lodgings which consist either of a house provided by the local authority or that of a private individual willing, for reward, to let his house for the accommodation of the judge. I have some personal experience of this for my father used to let his house outside Chester as the judge's lodgings and I remember how troublesome it was to have to turn out for the judge.

In most of the assize towns the ceremonial opening of the assize is preceded by a service in the parish church, in the course of which is said the Bidding Prayer. It is said with the congregation standing and, in form, varies from county to county. In Wiltshire it runs in this way—

THE BIDDING PRAYER
as used in the Church of St John the Baptist, Devizes

Ye shall pray for Christ's Holy Catholic Church, that is for the whole congregation of Christian peoples dispersed throughout the world; and especially for the Established Church of England; for the Queen's most excellent Majesty, our Sovereign Lady, Elizabeth, of the United Kingdom of Great Britain and Northern Ireland, and of the British Commonwealth beyond the seas, Queen, Defender of the Faith, over all persons supreme; also for Elizabeth,

The Queen Mother, Prince Philip, Duke of Edinburgh, Charles, Prince of Wales, and all the Royal Family.

Pray also for Ministers of God's Holy Word and Sacraments, as well Bishops, especially Joseph (Fison), Bishop of this Diocese, and Archbishops, especially Michael, Archbishop of Canterbury, Primate of all England and Metropolitan; also for the Queen's most honourable Council, for the High Court of Parliament, and for all the nobility of the Realm.

And, as in special duty bound, let us pray for Her Majesty's Judge of Assize, now on circuit in this County; for the High Sheriff of the County, and for the Mayor, and the Aldermen and Councillors of the Borough, that they may live in the faith and fear of God, in dutiful obedience to the Queen, and in brotherly charity to one another.

And that there may never be wanting a succession of persons duly qualified to serve God in Church and State, let us implore His blessing on all places of religious and useful learning, particularly on the Heads of Colleges and the Chancellors of Universities, that there and in all places set apart for God's honour and service, true religion and sound learning may flourish and abound.

To these prayers let us add unfeigned praise for mercies received in this place, for our creation, preservation and all the blessings of this life, particularly for the advantages afforded by the munificence of benefactors, such as Roger, Bishop of Salisbury; Matilda, Empress; Edward III, King; Thomas Thurman, Thomas Bancroft, Sir John and Dame Mary Eyles; Sidmouth, Viscount; Charles Henry Lowe and many others who have enriched this ancient Church and Borough.

Finally, let us praise God for all those departed this life in the faith of Christ, and pray unto God that we may have grace to direct our lives after their good examples; that, this life ended, we may be partakers with them of the glorious resurrection in the life everlasting; through Jesus Christ, our blessed Lord and Saviour.

Amen

Also in the course of the service the judges are appropriately reminded of the strict and solemn account which they themselves must one day give before the Judgment Seat itself.

In the judge's retinue is his clerk. In days gone by he was usually the judge's clerk in chambers while still at the Bar, but this has changed. A clerk with a busy set of chambers can make a very much larger income (often larger than some of the barristers he looks after) than he can as a judge's clerk. So, fairly recently, judge's clerks became civil servants. My clerk, Leonard Gullett, who looked after Mr Justice Byrne for a number of years, was the first ex-police officer to be appointed, having been a Detective-Inspector in Chelsea. The judge's clerk it is who makes the first announcement at the opening of the Commission to which I have referred already. He sits with the judge on the Bench, swears the witnesses and, of great importance, makes contact with the members of the Bar through their clerks, so as to facilitate the making up of each day's list of cases and in an effort to help as many people as possible. Since Leonard Gullett is the first individual to be mentioned here (and he has been a loyal aide for over ten years) may I express the hope that no-one who is referred to in this record will be in any way offended, since all such references are intended to be of a friendly nature.

It was said in this regard that the Countess of Oxford and Asquith—'Margot' to her friends—when she had written a book of memoirs referring intimately to many well-known and distinguished people, especially in the world of politics, wrote to the then Prime Minister, Mr Arthur Balfour—

My dear Arthur,
I do hope you do not mind the reference to yourself in the book.
Yours ever,
Margot

To this the Prime Minister replied—

My dear Margot,
What book?
Yours ever,
Arthur

In addition to the clerk, the judge may take a young man, usually on his way to the Bar, as his marshal. A marshal's duties are well described as similar to those of an A.D.C.

The judge also takes a butler and a cook, the latter to ensure that no poison is included in the judicial diet.

On the first working day of the assize, many personages do the judge the courtesy of calling upon him at his lodgings or of accompanying him to church or to the assize court itself. The High Sheriff of the county is always among those together with his chaplain. In many places also among them is the Lord Mayor, or Mayor, and Town Clerk, and, at some places, representatives of the nearby University.

In my experience people, apart from lawyers, know very little of the status and functions of the High Sheriff of a county although a joke about the Sheriff of Nottingham is inevitable if the subject is raised. It is said that the sheriff is the oldest secular dignitary under the Crown, the word coming from 'shire-reeve' or officer of the county. The origins of the shrievalty are admirably described in a most useful publication produced by *The Times* in 1961 entitled 'The High Sheriff', with an introduction by Mr Gavin Astor, one-time High Sheriff of Sussex.

It is, I believe, a customary courtesy of the office of the Lord Lieutenant of a county, to inform the High Sheriff if the Sovereign, or a member of the Royal Family, is visiting the county officially and the High Sheriff should assist the Lord Lieutenant in receiving the Royal visitor.

Among the other functions of the High Sheriff is attendance upon Her Majesty's judges of assize. This he discharges by accompanying the judge on the Bench, in uniform and with a sword, a symbol of the Queen's justice, which the High Sheriff has to execute upon malefactors, and with it, no doubt, to defend the person of the judge in case of need. It is customary in many places for the High Sheriff to provide footmen and trumpeters, the latter to produce a complimentary fanfare and warn the populace that the judge is approaching.

On the 14th April 1971 a meeting of High Sheriffs was called by Captain Jeremy Elwes whom I met when he was High Sheriff of Lincolnshire, to launch what *The Times* called 'a campaign to preserve the oldest office of the English Crown'. At this conference in London the High Shrievalty Association was formed to save the office of High Sheriff from disappearing when the Crown Court should replace the old Assize and Quarter Sessions Courts. A leading article in *The Times* was headed 'What will High Sheriffs do then?'

So long as custom requires that a High Sheriff should assist in receiving members of the Royal Family, there seems no reason for the office to disappear, but I suggest, and have so suggested to several High Sheriffs, that in a county no longer to be visited by High Court judges but to be visited by the new Circuit judges, the High Sheriff should attend the Circuit judge in a ceremonial way perhaps at the beginning of three of the four legal terms or at least once a year and on those days the High

Sheriff would have the opportunity of showing hospitality as he does at present. The High Sheriff's attendance upon the Circuit judge would I think be a duty agreeable to the High Sheriff and a fitting mark of the dignity and importance of the Circuit judge's office. A further suggestion as to the future functions of the High Sheriff came the other day from the Under Sheriff of Hertfordshire, Mr Nigel Longmore, whose family have held the office for 150 years. It was to the effect that Lords Lieutenant might consider inviting the High Sheriff during his year of office to undertake or share the duties in the county hitherto falling upon the Vice-Lieutenant.

While considering the functions and future of the High Sheriff, it is fitting to say a word of praise for the Under Sheriffs upon whom fall so many administrative duties. They are always of the utmost help to the High Sheriff and to the judge, and I owe a great deal to all of them for letting me have much material for this work.

CHAPTER II

The Bar of England and Wales

THE JUDGES of the High Court who attend the assizes, as well as nearly all other judicial figures, are chosen from the ranks of the Bar of England and Wales. Thus, it is of moment to say something about the Bar. Every Bar student must be a member of one of the four Inns of Court, and must keep the necessary number of terms by 'eating dinners', that is to say, dining in hall at his Inn on so many evenings in the Term. When an undergraduate I enjoyed 'eating dinners' at the week-end, returning to Oxford on Sunday evening by a train rather unconventionally named, which left Paddington about 10 o'clock, and had its counterpart from Liverpool Street to Cambridge. There are four Inns of Court: Lincoln's Inn, Gray's Inn, the Inner Temple and the Middle Temple, and each has a Royal Bencher.

There was a great occasion in 1949 when H.M. King George VI was Treasurer of the Inner Temple and H.M. Queen Elizabeth Treasurer of the Middle Temple. The King dined at the Middle Temple and the Queen presiding as Treasurer proposed his health. The reason why this joint dinner was held at the Middle Temple was that the Inner Temple Hall had not been restored after the grievous damage of the War.

H.M. Queen Elizabeth II dined with us at the Inner Temple on 21 December 1966 when H.R.H. Prince Philip was present.

It should be explained that the Treasurer of an Inn is, in effect, the chairman of the governing body which is composed of the Masters of the Bench. It is always hoped that each Inn will have a Royal Bencher. At the present time the Queen Mother is a Bencher of the Middle Temple, the Duke of Edinburgh of the Inner Temple, Princess Margaret of Lincoln's Inn and the Duke of Gloucester of Gray's Inn.

May I say a word or so about each of the four Inns.

Lincoln's Inn can be reached from Lincoln's Inn Fields,

Carey Street and Chancery Lane. In Chancery Lane until recently there was a splendid gatehouse dating from the time of Queen Elizabeth I and said to have been repaired from time to time by Ben Jonson then a bricklayer 'trowel in hand and book in pocket'. Alas the Gatehouse has been demolished. The Old Hall and the Chapel are distinguished buildings and the trees and lawns delightful; in New Square Charles Dickens worked for a time as a lawyer's clerk. The Old Hall was the Lord Chancellor's court historically and in literature the venue of Jarndice v. Jarndice and incidentally the court from which, in Iolanthe, the Lord Chancellor went out into Chancery Lane to shed a tear because he could not marry his own ward.

Gray's Inn, to the North of Holborn, was, as were the other Inns, much damaged by enemy action during the war, but the Hall and other buildings have been excellently restored. Francis Bacon was admitted as a student at the age of 15 and spent most of his life in Gray's Inn. Charles Dickens worked here too as an attorney's clerk in Gray's Inn Square.

On the South side of the Strand and Fleet Street lie the Inner and Middle Temples, divided by Middle Temple Lane which leads to the Embankment. Both Societies have charming gardens and delightful courts and lanes and together are owners and guardians of the Temple Church. In the Bidding Prayer, which is said there every Sunday during the legal Term, they are referred to as 'the two learned and honourable Societies of this House'.

The Temple Church in part dates from 1185. It escaped the Great Fire of 1666, but did not escape the savage bomb attacks upon the City of London on 1 May 1941 and was badly damaged.

It is often, and understandably, asked why this part of London within, but not part of, the City is called The Temple. The name derives from the Crusaders of the early twelfth century whose designation was the Order of Knights Templars. In the same century they built the New Temple on the bank of the Thames. Later, however, the Order was dissolved and the New Temple became the property of the Knights Hospitallers whose order was suppressed at the Reformation. The Crown then acquired the property, but certain lawyers had occupied parts of the building and were left undisturbed. In 1608 James I, by Charter, granted the freehold to the Masters of the Bench of

H.M. The Queen and
H.R.H. Prince Philip
dining at the Inner Temple
21 December 1966

the Inner Temple and the Middle Temple. It was a condition of the grant that the new proprietors should maintain the Temple Church for ever. The two Inns have been proud to do this so far for four centuries.

The learning and pure prose of the Master of the Temple, the Very Rev. Robert Milburn, formerly Dean of Worcester, give profound pleasure to his congregations. The singing of the Choir under the direction of that great figure in music, Dr George Thalben Ball, and his playing of the organ are indeed beautiful.

The Lamb and Flag is the device of the Middle Temple. According to John Stow, that Inn had not taken a device in 1631 and had the choice of the two Knights on one horse, or the Lamb and Flag. The Arms had, however, come into use by 1655 for they are mentioned in Matthew Carter's *Analysis of Honour* published in that year.

The Winged Horse Pegasus is the device of the Inner Temple. The first known reference to the Arms of the Inner Temple is in Gerard Lee's *Accedens of Armoury* published in 1562. In 1561 Lord Robert Dudley (afterwards Earl of Leicester) was the Lord Governor of the Inn's Christmas festivities. During the revels he dubbed twenty-five members of the Inn Knights of the Order of Pegasus. This was presumably a *jeu d'esprit* because he was at that time Master of the Horse.

On these matters relating to heraldry I went for guidance to a Bencher of the Inner Temple, Mr George Squibb, Q.C., Norfolk Herald, and he it was who told me about the two devices I have just described.

Many people are interested in heraldry—and how a coat of arms may be acquired is often odd. I remember when a benefactor presented a new and very fine oak roof for the refectory of Chester Cathedral, it was desired to incorporate in the roof the coats of arms of the Bishop, the City, the Lord Lieutenant and other dignitaries, and, of course, the Dean. The Dean, Bishop Norman Tubbs, was asked about his coat and said that he was very sorry but he was not armigerous. Undeterred, the architect caused to be carved a heraldic shield embracing three small tubs, and in this interesting way is perpetuated the memory of a well-loved cleric.

It will be remembered that, in outlining the history of the Temple, I recalled that, in 1608, the Benchers acquired the

The Temple Church, 1185

freehold of the property. Some may wonder who the Benchers were, and are. In each of the four Inns, senior members of the Bar or judges are elected Masters of the Bench, or, less formally, Benchers, and they govern their Inn under the chairmanship of the Treasurer.

It is said that a student from overseas, and there are many and all are warmly welcomed, sat for his examination and was to deal with a paper on Company Law. Among the questions this one appeared:

'What are debentures?'

to which our friend answered:

'De Benchers are de governing body of de Inn!'

It was on a similar occasion that the question was:

'What are the origins of the Common Law?'

to which came the answer:

'The origins of the Common Law are so ancient that they may be said to be lost in the mists of iniquity!'

Once called to the Bar, the barrister may go into chambers in one of the Inns of Court or in one of the big cities where there is a local Bar. I went to the local Bar in Liverpool and practised there, apart from the war years, until I took silk, that is became a King's Counsel.

A special problem presents itself in the case of a practising barrister who is also a Member of Parliament. I experienced this problem and for me it lasted for sixteen years and included the immediate post-war period, when one side or the other had very narrow majorities—6, 12, 18—so that one's attendance at the House was sternly required by the Whips. It sometimes brought about a ludicrous situation. Many, many times I have been opposed to Mr Sydney Scholefield Allen, Q.C., at, for example, the Liverpool Assize. He was a Labour member, having defeated that most agreeable Bencher of the Inner Temple, Sir Donald Somervell, afterwards Lord Somervell of Harrow, in a Parliamentary contest at Crewe. When there was a three-line Whip, Allen and I would solemnly board the train together at Lime Street, Liverpool, after our case had been adjourned, vote in opposite lobbies in the House and board the midnight train back to Liverpool. The only glimmer of sense about this was, I suppose, that one of us might have dropped dead, in which event the other side would be one vote better off—or is it mathematically two?

A frequent joke of the time was when one Member of the House would say to another:

'Have you heard that old so-and-so on the other side is ill?' to which the reply was:

'Dear me, dear me, nothing trivial I hope.'

Allen found difficulties, as I did, in seeking to practise the law and also be a politician, and it might be that he would sometimes chant—

> Oh Mr Attlee whatever shall I do
> I wanted to travel the Circuit
> But they put me IN at Crewe.

These difficulties were not only experienced by barristers who were members of the two major parties in the House. I remember Mr Roderick Bowen, Q.C., then the Liberal Member for Cardigan, coming to me about a fortnight after his election as a Member, and at the time when the total number of Liberal Members was six. He said:

'You know it is a most extraordinary thing, I now have four seats in our Shadow Cabinet.'

It was a great privilege to know that brilliant writer, now alas the late, Sir Alan Herbert otherwise 'A.P.H.'. He well understood the problems of the back bencher and I am grateful to his Estate for permitting me to include two of his verses which I found entertaining—

> Read Hansard for the papers cannot tell
> The many things that Parliament does well
> How many a Member labours many days
> To find his figures and perfect his phrase
> And waits and waits, while many a meal goes by
> Hungry and worn to catch the Speaker's eye
> Pours out his heart, his wisdom and his jokes
> And is enrolled among the Also Spokes

and the Politician's prayer—

> Aloft into the upper air
> Ascends the politician's prayer
> Grant me the gift of swift retort
> And keep the public memory short

In spite of the difficult problem involved for the practising barrister, I would not have missed my years in the House of Commons and always felt greatly honoured, and not a little surprised, that between 20,000 and 30,000 people should have voted for me at one election or another.

Of all those who took pride in membership of the House there stands out, I suppose, Sir Winston Churchill. In the early days of 1943 he came out to the Middle East and stayed at our Embassy in Cairo. Having been away from Parliament for two years I asked to see him. An appointment was made for 6 p.m., but, before then, a secretary telephoned to say:

'6 p.m. is not wholly suitable, could you possibly make it 6.45, but only if it is really convenient to you'.

How wonderfully diplomatic some of these permanent officials are. The Prime Minister was immensely kind, said that perhaps I should return for a time to Westminster, and told me frankly of his secret meeting with the Turks on a train in Northern Lebanon. Time went on, secretaries looked in and it ultimately appeared that General Wilson, 'Jumbo' as he was called, had been kept waiting for twenty minutes. The great man saw me out and in the hall introduced me to the General saying—

'This is Major Nield. He is a Member of Parliament', with that emphasis which left no doubt but that to be such was, indeed a high distinction. I too think it was.

To show again what a great House of Commons man Sir Winston Churchill was, I will always remember the debate after the Chamber of the House had been destroyed, as to the proposals for the re-building of the House. Many strange suggestions were made—for example, a large establishment twenty-five miles from London with squash courts, swimming pools and so on, but the Prime Minister strongly favoured re-building on the old site and in the old manner, and who else would have thought of concluding his speech as he did—

> Mid pleasures and palaces
> Tho' we may roam
> Be it ever so humble
> There's no place like home.

In the sombre years of the war the chimes of Big Ben were heard in the remotest parts of the world. I wonder if many of those who heard them knew that the tune is said to be based on a phrase in the accompaniment of Handel's 'I know that my Redeemer liveth' and traditionally spells out the message:

> Lord through this hour
> Be Thou our guide
> That by Thy power
> No foot shall slide

CHAPTER III

The Courts and the Judiciary

THE COURTS in England and Wales can be divided into two categories: those which exercise criminal jurisdiction and those which exercise civil jurisdiction.

On the criminal side there are three levels of courts. The first embraces the Central Criminal Court (commonly called the Old Bailey), the assizes sitting in the counties and two fairly recently constituted courts, the Crown Courts in Liverpool and Manchester. The second level embraces the Quarter Sessions for Boroughs and for Counties. The third level consists of the Courts of Petty Sessions or magistrates courts.

The Old Bailey takes its name from the narrow street which runs North from Ludgate Hill, which in turn takes its name from the Ballium, the defence wall which ringed the City of London. The Lord Mayor of London is the Chief Commissioner of the Court but the principal active judicial personage is the Recorder, whose historic office is now held by Sir Carl Aarvold, a great sportsman, universally liked and respected. Next in the hierarchy is the Common Serjeant, an office filled with distinction by Judge Mervyn Griffith-Jones. When Sir Anthony Hawke was Common Serjeant, he always referred to himself as the 'vulgar N.C.O.' Judges of the High Court attend at each session of the Central Criminal Court to deal with the gravest cases. The City of London is very generous in its provision of courts. The Central Criminal Court came into being as a result of a bill introduced by Lord Brougham in 1834. Since then many courts have been added and at this moment the number of courts is being greatly increased. Judge Jeffreys once held the office of Recorder of London and indeed he held several judicial offices of profit at one time or another. Whether his reputation as a savage judge is justified is open to doubt, but he was not always polite to witnesses and was very voluble.

The story is told that a witness described himself as a musician.

The Recorder asked: 'You are a fiddler, are you?'

Witness: 'My Lord, I am a violinist.'

Recorder: 'And what pray is the difference?'

Witness: 'About the same as the difference between a pair of bagpipes and a recorder'—adding under his breath—'and both are wind instruments.'

I recall Lord Justice Edmund Davies once defining a recorder as a rudimentary wind instrument 'and some are ruder than others'.

It was while I was sitting at the Old Bailey in 1963 that I was much complimented by the suggestion of the City Sheriffs that I might become a Freeman of the City of London (of course by redemption). They proposed me and I was most pleased to be sworn in.

The criminal jurisdiction of the assizes has already been referred to in Chapter I, but mention should be made of the two Crown Courts set up in 1956. For some years before 1956, it was found that at each assize in the two great centres of population in Lancashire, Liverpool and Manchester, so much of the time of the judge was taken up by the criminal work that the civil work fell very much into arrears. The judge's first task is always that of 'gaol delivery', that is to say to clear the gaols, so that civil suits were often delayed for a long time before being heard. A committee was appointed to see what steps could be taken to obviate these delays. I was a member of that committee, chosen, I think, in my capacity as Recorder of Salford. Had I had any idea that I might be asked to accept one of the new offices to be set up I suppose I would have had to resign. The committee's chief recommendation was that there should be established two new courts—one at each place—and that there should be created two new full-time judicial appointments to combine the duties of recorder and judge of the Crown Court. These courts were to exercise the jurisdiction formerly exercised by the criminal court at the assizes and also that of the City Quarter Sessions, the High Court judges dealing with the gravest cases as at the Old Bailey. This released the judge of assize for the despatch of the civil list of cases.

It was late one night at the House of Commons when the Attorney-General, Sir Reginald Maninngham-Buller, an old Oxford friend who later became Viscount Dilhorne and the Lord Chancellor, came to me in the Ayes lobby, at least I think it was there, and asked if I would take on the new post at Manchester. My heart sank a little because I was human enough to hope, and hope is the word and not expect, for appointment to the High Court. However, such a request cannot in the ordinary course be refused and so I accepted. I do not now regret it for a moment for I enjoyed to the full the four years during which I started and continued the new venture in Manchester. I shall always be grateful for the immense volume of kindness which I was shown by everyone with whom I came in contact and particularly for the wise guidance of the Clerk to my Court, Mr Ernest Edwards and his deputy, Mr George Jackson. I was much pleased that the Lord Chief Justice of England, Lord Goddard, came to open the new court. The then Lord Lieutenant of Lancashire, the Earl of Derby, was present and, at the insistence of the Lord Chief Justice, presided, taking precedence over all others as the Queen's permanent representative in the county. My suggestion that Lord Derby should take the more serious cases after lunch was rightly regarded as frivolous.

As time went on, I believe several other big cities, probably Birmingham among them, expressed a wish to have their own Crown Courts, but the Streatfeild Committee, to which reference has been made, recommended that—'more Crown Courts should not be set up at the present time'. Among the objections to the system of Crown Courts were the undesirability of a judge being always in the same court, and that he would be engaged upon criminal business all the time and might become prosecution-minded. The Beeching Committee was of the opinion that it was desirable that judges should move from place to place and take both criminal and civil cases.

I hope all my brother judges have noted with care the passage at paragraph 69 of the Beeching Report which reads—

> Movement of judges also has the advantage of ensuring that if they do occasionally develop idiosyncracies as a result of the exalted seclusion in which they live, their foibles move with them and do not become a source of irritation or amusement to any one section of the community.

The Northern Circuit had a large share of judicial appointments as the photograph on page 23 shows.

As to the second level of criminal courts, there are the

Borough Quarter Sessions presided over by a Recorder, who is a practising member of the Bar of standing and who sits every quarter, and more frequently if needed, and sits either alone or with assessors. There are also the County Quarter Sessions presided over by a Chairman, who is also a practising member of the Bar of standing, and who sits every quarter, or more frequently if needed, and sits with Justices of the Peace. These part-time judicial offices present many difficulties and a busy practitioner will be faced with a serious problem as to how to fit in the sittings of the court with his commitments as a practising member of the Bar.

The third level of criminal courts are the Courts of Petty Sessions at which sit the lay magistrates. There are I believe over 19,000 magistrates and they deal with the vast majority of the cases heard in all the courts in the land. Their jurisdiction extends, too, to civil matters such as domestic disputes of one kind and another. There is no doubt in my view that lay magistrates do invaluable work assisting in the administration of justice. It is the modern view that magistrates should receive a measure of instruction in their functions. This, no doubt, is admirable if it is not carried too far. The textbook largely relied upon in the magistrates court is *Stone's Justice Manual*. The word 'manual' is strange for it now runs into two closely printed volumes containing, I think, about 3,000 pages. My advice tentatively offered to Justices is:

'Do not hesitate to leave your Stone unturned. If a legal problem of difficulty arises, your clerk will be best able to resolve it.'

It was amusing to be told by a close friend who was a High Court judge, that his sister had recently been appointed a Justice of the Peace and had written to him as follows—

We had a difficult case before us yesterday. The defendant was charged with using obscene language. The nice policeman who prosecuted said that the words were so obscene he would prefer to write them down rather than repeat them. This was done and I found not only that I did not know what the words meant but I had never heard of them before. We fined the defendant 10/—do you think that was too much?

Turning to the courts exercising civil jurisdiction, there are two levels: the High Court and the County Courts, the latter

Northern Circuit judges, October 1962

Back row: Mocatta, J., Barry, J., Nield, J., Thompson, J., Gorman, J., Ashworth, J., Fenton Atkinson, J., Brabin, J.

Front row: Willmer, L.J., Sellers, L.J., Lord Morris of Borth-y-Gest, Ormerod, L.J., Lloyd-Jacob, J.

dealing with the less weighty cases. The High Court established at the Royal Courts of Justice in the Strand, is divided into three divisions: the Chancery Division of which the Lord Chancellor is titular head—the administrative side, in fact, is dealt with by the Vice-Chancellor, at present Sir John Pennycuick; the Queen's Bench Division, having as its head the Lord Chief Justice of England; and thirdly, the Probate, Divorce and Admiralty Division (as it is called at the moment, but the name of which is to be changed to the Families Division), the head of which has recently been appointed Sir George Baker.

All judges must be deeply conscious of the grave issues with which they must deal but occasionally one is able to look upon the lighter side. A judge sitting in a divorce suit told me not long ago how the evidence indicated trouble caused by the in-laws of one of the spouses. The husband, it was said, had docked the tail of his highly-bred pedigree dog and was asked why on earth he had done this. He said:

'My mother-in-law is coming to stay with us next week and I am determined that there shall not be the slightest sign of welcome.'

It is recommended that all County Court judges should become Circuit judges when the new arrangements come into force.

At present there is an appeal from the magistrates to Quarter Sessions; from the High Court to the Court of Appeal, consisting of the three Lords Justices of Appeal; and from the Court of Appeal to the House of Lords, the tribunal being composed of the Lords of Appeal in Ordinary. Judges at any level are, I think, interested, and sometimes concerned, as to the outcome of appeals against their decisions. In the days when the old Court of Criminal Appeal sat on a Monday, at Tuesday's breakfast table on circuit it was always noticeable how the judges turned hastily to the page of Law Reports in *The Times* to see how they had got on the day before. It was said of Mr Justice Swift that meeting Lord Justice Scrutton in the corridor at the Law Courts, the latter said:

'Well Rigby we've had to upset you again,'
to which the reply was—

'Upset, certainly not. I may be reversed, but upset never'.

With an increasing number of judicial appointments, it may well become difficult to find members of the Bar of the right calibre to fill them and, quite naturally, the question has again been raised as to the appointment of members of the other branch of the profession, solicitors, to judicial office. It is, of course, the case that many solicitors have transferred to the barristers' branch, and indeed members of the Bar are often disbarred at their own request in order to become solicitors. Many High Court judges have begun their lives in the Law as solicitors. Mr Justice Lynskey was one and I think he was a very great judge. Lord Justice Ormerod, now retired, was another. He had a remarkable career, starting as an articled clerk and becoming in turn a solicitor, a member of the Bar, a County Court judge, a judge of the High Court in the Probate, Admiralty and Divorce Division, a judge of the Queen's Bench Division and, finally, a Lord Justice of Appeal. The House of Lords, I feel, would have been strengthened by his presence, but sadly the years go by. Mr Justice Payne's career so far is similar to that of Lord Justice Ormerod. The present Lord Chief Justice, Lord Widgery, also started as a solicitor.

When the first woman came to be appointed a judge of the High Court—and it was Dame Elizabeth Lane, formerly a County Court judge—a problem presented itself as to her proper designation and how she was to be addressed in court. At first it seemed to be agreed that she should be called '*Mr* Justice' and addressed as 'My Lord'. It was, however, represented to Lord Gardiner, then Lord Chancellor, that this was really quite inappropriate. The first alternative advanced was '*Madam* Justice' and to be addressed as 'My Lady' with which I agreed. In the end the decision was to call her '*Mrs* Justice'—this in spite of the obvious problem if the holder of the office should be unmarried. '*Miss* Justice' does not somehow sound quite right.

In all this, the unattractive question of judicial salaries cannot be ignored. The salary of a High Court judge stayed as it was, when it was fixed in 1832, until 1954. When it was fixed, it was sufficient to enable the judge to live in suitable style and to be free from financial anxiety of any kind. Times changed and Lord Simmons, when Lord Chancellor, had the invidious task of putting the case for an increase. In this he was successful. It may or may not be true that one of those against any increase pointed out that the original salary was put high so that the judge would not be tempted to take any bribe, but now, he argued, there is no possibility of any member of the judiciary taking a bribe, so why increase the salary?

It is apposite to notice that Mr Henry Cecil, otherwise Judge Leon, whom I am glad to know and whose books have given so much pleasure, wrote one in quite a serious vein on the subject of possible corruption of the judiciary which, with his remarkable flair for titles, he called '*Tipping the Scales*'.

CHAPTER IV

The South-Eastern Circuit

O<small>N THE</small> South-Eastern Circuit assizes were held in nine
towns—
> Cambridge
> Chelmsford
> Hertford
> Maidstone
> Norwich
> Bury St Edmunds
> Ipswich
> Kingston-upon-Thames
> Lewes

As will be seen, most of these towns are within easy reach of
London. This results in the South-Eastern Circuit having much
less circuit life than other circuits. On most circuits members
of the Bar stay in the recognized Bar hotel in the assize town in
question. They dine together in Bar Mess, having their own wine
cellar, silver and often their own butler. The South-Eastern
Circuit, however, have a dinner at the end of the year to which
the judges who have visited them are invited—and which is
always an enjoyable occasion.

CAMBRIDGE

As Dr Helen Cam has written:

> The earliest mention of Cambridge is by Bede. He tells how in
> 695 monks from Ely found a stone coffin for St Etheldreda's bones
> in 'a little ruined city near the Granta'.

He called it Grantchester. When the Danes occupied the
town in 875 it was called Granta Bridge.

There have been local courts in Cambridge for nearly 1,000
years. According to the historians, the shire and the town had
their own courts in the eleventh century. The town court was

for freemen only and exercised capital jurisdiction for 200 years. This court was succeeded by a court for all the people presided over by the Mayor and Bailiffs, and this lasted until the establishment of the modern County Court about 500 years later.

The assizes have certainly been held in Cambridge since 1298, but I think it is clear that they were held as early as 1261. It will be remembered that, as recently as 1970, a number of 'students' (it seems to be almost as if the present troubles started when they ceased to be called undergraduates) were sentenced to imprisonment for riotous behaviour at the Garden House Hotel. This was by no means the first instance of violent behaviour on the part of members of the University.

In *Cooper's Annals for 1261* there is the following passage—

1261

A north country and a south country scholar had some words which ended in blows, upon which a general affray commenced between the two parties, and in which the townsmen joined: the greatest confusion prevailed; every description of outrage was committed; the houses of either party were plundered, and the records of the University burnt. Upon the news of these tumults being brought to the King, he issued commissions for the trial of the offenders. The first commission was directed to Giles Argentein, Henry de Borham, and Lawrence de Broke; but it being suggested that their conduct was not impartial, another commission with limited powers was awarded to Nicholas de Turr and Nicholas de Handlo, the justices itinerant. Ultimately, however, the matter was remitted to the commissioners first appointed. Sixteen townsmen were executed, many on either side received slighter punishments of various kinds, others fled to sanctuary, and twenty-eight southern scholars obtained the King's pardon.

Anxious to escape from the tumults then so frequently occurring here, a number of the more peaceable and studious scholars joined a party of students who had left Oxford for similar reasons, and obtained the King's license to establish a University at Northampton, to which town they accordingly removed.

In March 1461 it is recorded that King Edward IV attended the assizes in Cambridge and was much gratified by the charge of the presiding judge, Sir William Yelverton, to the Sheriffs and other officers, so much so that he asked him to deliver a similar charge at the Norfolk Assizes.

Disease and tempest seem to have struck the Cambridge Assizes from time to time. In 1521, the assize being then for long before and long after held at the Castle, the justices and all the gentlemen, bailiffs and others resorting to the assizes fell victim to an infectious disease. Many died and others became seriously ill Cooper was uncertain whether the infection was due to 'the savour of the prisoners or the filth of the house.'

Just forty years later there were plans to build courts for assizes and sessions, the resolution reading—

> Lord Northe shall and maie build a house where ye fishe stalls do nowe stand within the market place of the towne of Cambridge, of such lengthe and breadythe as the grounde there maie bere, for ye Justices of the Assyses & Sessions to syt in assises and sessions, so that the comoditie thereof maie ryse to the benefyt of the towne. And that the sea fishe shall from the feaste of Easter next, be solde in the lane called Pumpe Lane & in no other place of the streats, for ye avoidinge of the noysance that maie ryse therebye to the Justices in their syttings there & the inhabitants of the towne.

These courts were never built.

In 1630, because of the Plague, the summer assize was held at Royston instead of Cambridge.

In 1666, owing to the inclemency of the weather in March, the Crown Court sat at the Town Hall and the Nisi Prius Court in the Borough Market instead of at the Castle.

In 1747 a Shire House was built next to the Tolbooth or Guildhall. It fronted on to the market place and was built on pillars, market stalls being erected under the first floor. This building was used for the assizes and County Sessions until 1842 when the assize courts, which were demolished in 1961, were erected on Castle Hill. In 1817 the Shire House had been recently painted and

> 'the smell was so offensive that the judges refused to hold the summer assizes there and the Nisi Prius Court was held at St John's College Hall and the Crown Court at Jesus College Hall'.

In recent times the assizes have sat at the Guildhall.

The assize service is held at the University Church at Great St Mary's in King's Parade and the custom of preaching an assize sermon there probably dates from the Reformation. The Assize Bell was rung before the sermon from early times until the present century. In 1672 it is recorded that the sermon was preached at 7 a.m.

The Master's Lodge, Trinity College, Cambridge

Procession at Cambridge (in order of procession): Colonel Douglas Kaye (High Sheriff), L. Gullett (clerk), Nield, J., Andrew Geddes (marshal), A. C. B. Laker

It is to be noticed that in Bridge Street is St Sepulchre's Church, one of the very few round churches in the Kingdom; another one, as has been mentioned, is the Temple Church, which follows the design of the Church of the Holy Sepulchre in Jerusalem.

At one time pairs of gloves were presented to the judge by the Vice-Chancellor and the Mayor. This agreeable custom has ceased. Earlier, too, there are records of handsome gifts of food, such as Judge Leon has recalled. For example, on a day in 1664 there were delivered to the judge's lodgings—

1 veale
1 Sheepe
1 Pike
2 Ducks
2 Eales
6 Perches.

There was a time, it would seem, when the judges of assize were housed at Barnwell Abbey. However, certainly since the time of James I, and perhaps before, the judge has been housed in the Master's Lodge at Trinity College. Professor P. W. Duff, the Vice-Master of Trinity, tells me that the custom goes back to the personal friendship of Edward Coke, the judge, and Thomas Nevile, the Master under James I. The judge's quarters consist of the Master's large and beautiful dining room on the ground floor and a wing with bedrooms. It must be inconvenient for the Master to relinquish his dining room in this way. I have been fortunate enough to go twice to Cambridge, on both occasions during the Mastership of Lord Butler of Saffron Walden whom of course I knew well in my political days. I was much pleased to be able to entertain him and Lady Butler to dinner under their own mahogany and also to dine with the Master at the High Table and to drink port afterwards in the Senior Common Room.

For the future the proposal is that in Cambridge there should be a Crown Court served by Circuit judges only.

CHELMSFORD

In the county town of Essex, before the opening of the assize, the service is held at the parish church of St Mary's which was rebuilt in 1428 and again in 1800 and is now the cathedral.

The Shire Hall, Chelmsford

The courts are held in the Shire Hall, an elegant building begun in 1789 and it is to be noticed that in the Square is a bronze statue of Lord Chief Justice Tindal, who is referred to elsewhere in this record and who was born in Chelmsford.

When the office of Sheriff was instituted, those first appointed for Essex exercised authority also over Hertfordshire. From some notes which I have, made by the late Mr Henry Hamilton Gepp a former Under Sheriff, I learn that harsh things were sometimes said of sheriffs and judges. About 1100 Henry of Huntingdon says: 'Sheriffs and judges were the most cruel of all tyrants and greater plunderers than common thieves and robbers.'

It was Henry II who restored the Earldom of Essex to a de Mandeville. The Earl in those days was virtually the Governor of the county; he held courts, the Sheriff being merely his deputy. It was at this time, however, that the King appointed itinerant justices to go on circuit through the country. The first Essex Assizes sat at Brentwood. The sittings were migratory; in 1285 they were at Chelmsford and in 1568 at Witham.

The Court of Justice Leat (the highest forest court) held by the Lord Chief Justice under the King's Commission first sat at Chelmsford and afterwards at Chigwell.

Judges' procession at Chelmsford, 2 August 1762

In the reign of Richard II, a court was opened at Chelmsford for the trial of those concerned in the Wat Tyler rebellion.

In 1645 the Earl of Warwick, the High Sheriff assisted by various justices held a court at Chelmsford to try witches.

The judges' lodgings are near to the court in a very good house with a large garden. The judges' procession in fine weather goes on foot to the court.

Chelmsford is so near London that counsel travel to and fro daily and many young members of the Bar visit an assize court for the first time at Chelmsford, and indeed often have their first High Court briefs there. In these circumstances to the inexperienced, I venture, with some diffidence, to offer a few words of advice as to advocacy in general and manners in court in particular.

It sometimes seems as if there are, broadly speaking, two categories of advocates: those who are 'fortiter in modo' and those who are 'suaviter in modo'. In the first category come those who cross-examine something like this: with wagging forefinger raised

'I put it to you that you are an unmitigated liar.'

In the years that I have been in the profession of the Law I have never heard the witness answer

'Yes, as a matter of fact I am.'

Thus I would recommend the suaviter approach.

It is elementary that the advocate should speak up. It is equally important that he should stand up. Sometimes difficulties arise. On the Northern Circuit years ago there were two distinguished counsel, Mr Alfred Kennedy who was about 5 ft. 2 and Sir Ernest Wingate-Saul (father of the present County Court judge) who was about 6 ft. 7. Appearing against each other Mr Kennedy for the plaintiff started to open his case—

The judge interposed: 'Please, Mr Kennedy, stand up when you address the Court.'

Mr Kennedy: 'My Lord, I am standing up.'

The judge: 'Well then Sir Ernest, please sit down when your opponent is addressing the Court.'

'My Lord' said Sir Ernest 'I am sitting down.'

'Oh dear' said the judge, 'I apologize to you both.'

When reading a document I would say to counsel: always hold it up to eye level and never leave it on the desk and bend over it so that all the court sees is the top of your head. Further, and on a different point, if a document is handed to you for the first time, look at both sides. Quite often I have known litigants make most damaging notes on the back of a document which they do not expect to have to disclose.

As for manners, well plainly one does not address the Court with hands in pockets; still less jingling coins or keys in the pocket. Similarly, to engage your opponent or others in whispered conversation, particularly when the judge is summing up or giving judgment, is far from courteous. The foot on the seat beside you, the gown in careful disarray slipping from the shoulder, the monocle of plain glass will really avail you very little; posturing gains scant reward.

How far counsel makes notes must be a matter for him. Serjeant Sullivan, the last of the Serjeants, in court never untied the red tape from his brief, yet knew the name and address of every witness and what his proof of evidence was. On the other hand, a Leader on the Northern Circuit made the most copious notes with detailed stage directions in the margin, for example—

Here take out handkerchief
Here remove spectacles with flourish
Here pause for effect
Here weep

The successful advocate I think is one who has apparently an intense belief in the righteousness of his cause and presents his case with courtesy and economy of words. It is said that, on one occasion in the Court of Appeal, counsel stood for a day behind an immense pile of documents, including about 500 pages of correspondence, and on the second day said—

'My Lords, I now propose to read the correspondence,' at which Lord Goddard, who was presiding, commented loudly but not loudly enough to reach the shorthand note—

'Not on your life, Mr so and so.'

Again, counsel must obey the rules; one of which is when examining his own witness not to put leading questions, a leading question being, as few laymen realize, one which suggests the answer. A member of the Bar on the South-Eastern Circuit once went a little far. He was asking questions of his client, who was the driver of a car involved in a collision:

'When you reached the cross-roads what did you do?'
Answer—'I slowed down.'
Question: 'What else?'
Answer—'I looked both ways.'
Question: 'What else?'
'Well I think that was all.'
Counsel—'Now, now, what else did you do?'
Answer—'Nothing I think.'
Counsel—'Come, come, did you blow your nose?'
Answer—'Oh, no, I blew my horn.'
Counsel—'That's better.'

Sir Noel Goldie of the Northern Circuit was supremely careful not to ask leading questions and was known to say to the lady driver:

'Now Madam, tell me if you will be so good—and I do not want to lead you in any way, so answer the question Yes or No—which side of the road were you driving on?'

Sir Noel's real claim to fame made in the days of juries was that he had won more cases at first instance and lost them in the Court of Appeal than any other Leader on his circuit.

Having ventured to make a few remarks about advocacy and

the behaviour of counsel, it is perhaps fair to say a word or so about the attitude of judges to counsel. One of the great temptations on the Bench is to ask questions instead of waiting to see if counsel do not ask them. Indeed to listen and watch and wait might be a useful guide to anyone exercising judicial functions. But of all the qualities that rightly appeal to counsel, and I think to the public, courtesy is paramount. When the Attorney-General, Sir Peter Rawlinson, bade farewell to Lord Parker on his retirement from the office of Lord Chief Justice, he made this point having in mind Lord Parker's almost persistent courtesy in his many years on the Bench. In my young days, those whom I really enjoyed appearing before on this account were Viscount Finlay and Mr Justice Lawrence, later Lord Trevethin and Oaksey. It will be remembered that Lord Oaksey presided at the Nuremburg trials. Many I think disapproved of the War Crimes trials, but, and I have no doubt of this, never at any time has the British judiciary stood higher both in the estimation of the public and in the estimation of the war-time Allies. It is a fact that whenever any point arose, whenever any problem presented itself, the Americans, the French and the Russians looked to the British team for guidance and that guidance was without hesitation accepted.

To return to Essex, for the future the proposal is that in Chelmsford there should be a Crown Court served by High Court and Circuit judges.

HERTFORD

The assize court is held in the Town Hall, which was re-built in 1771. Originally it was in the Castle but, by a Charter of James I in 1606, there was granted to the Borough a Town Hall, reserving its use to the King for the 'Sessions of the Peace to be held in the County as hath been used'.

The judge's lodgings are a private house, the house of a friend of mine, Mr Mark Chapman-Walker, who has converted an old mill near Ware most attractively. The mill is very near the home of Mr Justice Chapman.

Mr Chapman-Walker was at one time a senior figure at the Conservative Central Office and we often met at the House of Commons—sometimes for dinner in the Harcourt room. It was there that two American guests were being entertained when,

West Mill, near Ware

about half-way through dinner, the division bell rang out loudly
all over the building and Members hurried out to vote. Left
alone, one American guest said to the other:
'Say, what do you think that is?'
and his companion replied:
'I guess one of them's escaped.'
The sittings of the courts in Hertford have a long and interest-
ing history. In the Patent Rolls in the thirteenth, fourteenth and
fifteenth centuries, there are constant references to hearings at
Hertford. For a number of years in the sixteenth century the
Law Courts were evacuated from London on account of the
Plague and sat in the Castle at Hertford.
A number of remarkable trials are recorded.
In 1629 three persons were tried for the murder of a woman
and acquitted. The judge disapproved of the verdict and ordered
that the body be exhumed. The accused were required to touch
the body and, when they did so, the eyes opened three times and
blood dropped from one of its fingers. The accused were re-tried
and two of them were convicted and hanged.
In 1712 one Jane Wenham was found guilty of 'Conversing

with the Devil in the shape of a cat'. She was sentenced to death but was reprieved 'amid a flood of pamphleteering'.

In 1751 Thomas Colley was found guilty of murdering Ruth and John Osborn by drowning. They had been thrown into a pond at Tring by way of a test for witchcraft.

In 1823 John Thurball was condemned to death for the murder of William Weare over a gambling debt. The trial caused a national sensation and a campaign to demonstrate the evils of gambling.

As recently as 1876 there was a public execution—the last there—at the gaol in Ware Road, a gaol which was closed two years later.

It is sad that with so long and colourful a history the assizes at Hertford will end.

For the future the new proposal is that in Hertford there should be a Crown Court served by High Court and Circuit judges, but only until courts are available at Luton.

MAIDSTONE

Before the middle of the eighteenth century, the Kent Assizes were held in a number of places in the county—Dartford, Gravesend, Greenwich and Sevenoaks—but, by that time, Maidstone had become the main assize town.

Richard Kilburne's *Topographie 1659* contains this passage relating to Maidstone—

> The Town is accounted the Shire Town, and the Assizes for the County have (in the time of the late King Charles and since) been holden here above ten times oftner, and (in the time of the late King James) three times oftner than in all other places of the County.

From the late sixteenth century the Maidstone Assizes were held in a courthouse on the site of the present Town Hall. In 1608 a further courthouse was built. This was replaced by the present Town Hall in the middle of the eighteenth century. The Sessions House, now incorporated in the County Hall, was built in 1825 and the present courts were used as assize courts for the first time in December 1827.

The town seems to have been prominent in several rebellions. It is said that Wat Tyler was a native of Maidstone and that in 1381 his supporters over-ran the town, forced a way into the

The old Lodgings, Maidstone

Archbishop's prison and rescued John Ball, called sometimes 'the mad priest of Kent' and the author of the lines:

'When Adam delved and Eve span,
Who was then a gentleman?'

In 1450 Jack Cade's rebellion found support in the town.

In 1554 Thomas Wyatt's rebellion occurred and he himself was later executed.

As was often the case up and down the country, the holding of the assizes was an occasion which brought many people to the town and personages from the county and Justices of the Peace, some of them forming a Grand Jury, met to discuss matters of local interest. It was in fact during the Spring Assize of 1642 that the famous Kentish Petition to Parliament was drawn up, its rejection being one of the factors leading to the Civil War.

Some notable trials have taken place at Maidstone in the past.

In 1765 prisoners in Maidstone gaol rioted and killed a gaoler and seriously wounded the Chaplain and they were tried by a special assize court in November of that year.

In 1798 a treason trial was held when two Irishmen, captured in Kent, were tried after trying to escape to revolutionary France with messages from English sympathizers. The trial was attended by several leading politicians, including Charles James Fox.

I do not know if Kent is really antipathetic to lawyers, but it

Wierton Grange, near Maidstone

was in Maidstone, I think at a Law Society dinner, that a speaker told the story of a lawyer named Strange. As he approached 70—that is, I like to think, early middle age—he thought it time to consider the sort of headstone which he wished to be placed over his grave. He chose the stone and said

'Inscribe upon it simply these words "Here lies a lawyer and an honest man".'

'No name?' asked the stonemason.

'No name,' he said. 'Anyone passing will read this "Here lies a lawyer and an honest man" and will say "That's Strange".'

The sequel however is even more pointed. When the lawyer died and was duly buried beneath his stone, two friends passed by and read the inscription and one said to the other

'I wonder why they buried two of them in the one grave.'

The judge's lodging in Maidstone used to be the Stonehouse, in Lower Stone Street, dated 1716 but part of it being much earlier. Recently however it has been at Wierton Grange, Boughton Monchelsea, some six miles from the town.

For the future the proposal is that in Maidstone there should be a Crown Court served by High Court and Circuit judges.

NORWICH

Again, one finds the history of an assize town going back for centuries. In Norman times Norwich developed rapidly, and the great Cathedral, where the assize service has hitherto been held, was begun in 1096. Norwich was made a County of a City in the reign of King Henry IV and so has had a separate Commission as a City since then. Until 1837 the Lent Assizes for the County were held at Thetford but the Norfolk and Norwich Association Assizes Act 1832 provided that both the County Assizes should be held in Norwich and that the City should have two assizes a year. In recent years it has been the practice for the City Assize to be formally opened at the Guildhall and then adjourned to the Shirehouse where the two Assizes are in effect amalgamated.

The present Shirehouse was built in 1823. One reads in the *East Anglian* newspaper of twenty-five years ago that, in the eighteenth century, the leading citizens of Norwich, reinforced by the gentry from the county, were accustomed to enjoy a week of fashionable assemblies, concerts, balls, play actings and tea drinkings, upon what now seems the curious pretext, that it was Assize Week: and if any county gentleman had no business at the assizes, then it behoved him to invent some for the benefit of his womenfolk who would not be absent from the fashionable enjoyments. It appears from Mackerell's *History of Norwich 1732* that the City Assizes attracted similar merrymaking.

Clear it is that much pageantry surrounded the appearance of Her Majesty's judges to take the assizes. The *Eastern Evening News* some forty odd years ago described the procession which set out to meet the judges in 1839.

The City Sheriff decorated with the gold chain of office, in a full bodied carriage drawn by four fine greys, preceded on foot by eight officers in dark blue liveries and gold laced hats with white wands.

The High Sheriff and his brilliant cortège headed by about forty of the worthy baronet's tenantry on horseback wearing red and yellow favours, then followed on foot by two trumpeters and twenty javelin men, the marshal and the Under Sheriff and, lastly, Sir Thomas Hare, in full Court dress in his coach and four accompanied by his Chaplain.

The Cathedral, Norwich

The Courts, Norwich

The Coach, Norwich

Much of such pageantry has already disappeared; more will go.

One of the special interests of an assize in Norfolk is the use by the judge of a coach. Two magnificent shire horses draw the coach with the 'Red judge' as a passenger from the Cathedral to the courts. The horses are, I understand, kindly lent by a nearby brewery.

From Norwich it was an easy journey to visit my elder sister, Mrs J. W. E. Dickson, at Dunwich.

It may have been at Norwich that two moments, in the course of dealing with civil business, have remained in my memory.

The first was when a plaintiff, who was seeking damages for personal injuries including concussion, said—

'The first thing I remember, my Lord, after being knocked down was when I woke up in hospital unconscious!'

The second was when a very young counsel was cross-examining a witness in a motor collision case, the witness being a solid and respectable farm labourer. His evidence had been

The author's sister, Mrs J. W. E. Dickson, Mrs Greenway and Melford
Stevenson, J. at Norwich

Tower House, Bracondale, Norwich

highly damaging to the plaintiff, since he said that, after the accident, the plaintiff approached him and said:

'Oh, dear, it was all my fault.'

Somehow or other the defendants' counsel had to cast doubt on this evidence and, wisely, was endeavouring to suggest that the plaintiff, through his injuries, was in no fit state to know what he was saying. The question to the farm labourer, however, was as follows—

'I put it to you, Mr Robinson, that it must have been clear beyond peradventure that my client was suffering from retrograde amnesia at the time.'

The witness said—

'Eh?'

From about 1901 the county took a house in the Close for the judge's lodgings. It was hired from Dr Bates, the Cathedral organist, and, when he left in 1928, direct arrangements were made with the Dean and Chapter, who let the house to a solicitor from Norwich subject to its use for the judges. After 1943 this arrangement ceased. In 1947 the County Council succeeded in buying the distinguished Georgian house, the Tower House, Bracondale, which had been lived in during the war by the Bishop of Norwich, his Palace having been requisitioned. The first judge to occupy the house was Sir Reginald Croom-Johnson, whose son was appointed a judge of the High Court in 1971.

For the future the proposal is that in Norwich there should be a High Court and a Crown Court served by High Court and Circuit judges.

BURY ST EDMUNDS

Bury St Edmunds was made a Royal town of East Anglia by the Saxons. Its present name is derived from St Edmund the King and Martyr who was put to death by the Danes in 870. In 1020 a monastery was founded there by Canute, which, it is said, for its magnificence and splendour surpassed every other establishment of the kind in Britain with the exception of Glastonbury.

The abbot of the day had great power. He could inflict capital punishment and was also the judge in civil causes within the liberty. The privilege of coining was granted to the abbot by Edward the Confessor.

St Edmundsbury Cathedral

Barton Court, near Bury St Edmunds

The assizes for the County of Suffolk are held alternately at Bury St Edmunds and at Ipswich, and at Bury the court sits in the Shirehall. The judge's lodgings are at Barton Court, some three miles from the centre of the town and owned by the county. It is a little difficult to find the house through the attractive Suffolk lanes and directions from the locals are not always easy to follow. The usual sort of thing is:

'First on the left past the Red Lion. Second to the right and left at the fork. You simply can't miss it!'

One of my friends always used a variant of the last few words, namely:

'You simply can't *help* missing it.'

Bury St Edmunds has a special place in my regard since it was the last of the sixty-one towns which I was to visit and I had to wait for the opportunity to do so for quite a time. It was not unknown to many of my brother judges that, having been to the other sixty towns, this was the one I must reach soon, and when I was at last able to choose to go to Bury St Edmunds, there were agreeable murmurs at the judges' meeting of 'Well done, full house.'

Mr Commissioner John May (now May, J.), Lady May at Barton Court,
near Bury St Edmunds

For the future the proposal is that in Bury St Edmunds there will (subject to a temporary arrangement to alternate with Ipswich) be magistrates' courts only.

IPSWICH

Suffolk's largest town, Ipswich, has been of importance for a long time. It stands close to the estuary of the Gipping and the town's name comes from Gippy, originally spelt Gippesiwic. Immediately before the Norman Conquest Ipswich was in the possession of Edith, wife of Edward the Confessor and sister of Harold. The Normans built a castle there and King John granted the burgesses their first charter in 1200.

Belstead House, Ipswich

Two famous residents must be specially mentioned: Cardinal Wolsey, who was born in a house near St Nicholas Church, his father being described as either a tavern keeper or a butcher; and Sir Christopher Milton, a seventeenth-century poet who lived and died in the town, who was a brother of John Milton, became deputy recorder of Ipswich and later a judge.

A new Courthouse has been built in Civic Drive and was opened on 25 September 1968 by the Lord Chancellor, Lord Hailsham of St Marylebone. There are here four courts and excellent arrangements for the Bar, solicitors, jurors, witnesses and the public.

The judges' lodgings have been at Belstead House, a little way from the town and used I believe, by the Education Authority for residential courses and the training of students. Regretfully, I record that it is sometimes quite unfairly, but in good-humoured jest, referred to as Belsen.

For the future the proposal is that in Ipswich there will (subject to a temporary arrangement to alternate with Bury St Edmunds) be a Crown Court served by Circuit judges only.

KINGSTON-UPON-THAMES

The assizes for the County of Surrey originally sat at Guildford, but there was much adverse criticism from the judges of the accommodation there. On 29 June 1928, Mr Justice Avory was blunt in his criticism and took the opportunity to make his views known by addressing the Grand Jury (Grand Juries were then still in being) in these words—

> On the last occasion on which I addressed the Grand Jury here, I expressed the hope that within a reasonable time accommodation for the holding of the Assizes would be provided here in Guildford of a character more suitable and more consistent with the standing and traditions of this county than this place, which is a makeshift appurtenance of a cinema.

On the same occasion Mr Justice Avory noted, but did not agree with, the suggestion that the assizes should be transferred to Kingston-upon-Thames and held in the County Hall there. Much consultation took place and the judges of the King's Bench Division expressed a preference for Guildford, the seat of the Bishopric; and improvements to the Guildhall at Guildford were suggested. In the end, however, improvements in the County Hall at Kingston were agreed to and, by an Order in Council dated 15 May 1930, the assizes were moved from Guildford to Kingston-upon-Thames where they were first held in July 1930.

Talbot Lodge, Esher

Kingston has a very long and interesting history. The first recorded reference to the town is dated 838 when King Edward held a great Council there. Kingston has considerable privileges, including its own trade regulations by Gild; its own coroners; the right to debar the County Sheriff from local jurisdiction; and the right to elect its own High Steward and Recorder. There are no Quarter Sessions for the Borough so that the Recorder, at present my friend Sir Elwyn Jones, lately the Attorney-General, is not overburdened. The emoluments, however, which the office carries is the gift of two sugar loaves.

In 1927 King George V confirmed for Kingston its title of a Royal Borough, a proud distinction, since there are only three other Royal Boroughs in England and Wales—Windsor, Kensington and Chelsea, and Caernarvon.

The judge's lodgings are at Esher, an attractive house called Talbot Lodge, and when the Under Sheriff, Mr David Longdon, wrote to me not long ago he said:

'I am pleased to report that the colony of badgers still appears to be in existence on the hill adjoining Talbot Lodge.'

For the future the proposal is that in Kingston-upon-Thames there should be a Crown Court served by Circuit judges only.

George Lambert (marshal) and the author at Lewes

LEWES

In Saxon times there existed in Lewes a Merchand Gild which then served to protect the trading privileges of its members and to maintain standards. It was King Athelstan who prohibited the coining of money except in certain principal towns of the Kingdom; Lewes was one of the few towns to be allowed two mints.

The members of the Merchand Gild appear to have reconstituted themselves as the Society of Twelve and the records dating from 1542 show that the members comprised 'The wealthier and discreter sort of townsmen' who traditionally regulated the affairs of the town through their appointed officers. The duties of these officers were concerned with the Law. Part of the rate then levied was for the maintenance of the Sessions House and other commitments included the apprehension and imprisonment of malefactors, the whipping of rogues and beggars and the suppressing of civil disorder.

In 1812 the old Sessions House was demolished and replaced by the present County Hall.

The earliest surviving Assize Roll in the Public Record Office which refers to the court being held at Lewes is dated

The County Hall, Lewes

1248, although it is likely that assizes had in fact been held here at an earlier date. In addition to Lewes, East Grinstead, Horsham and Chichester have all been at one time or another the venue for the assizes for Sussex. Since 1748, however, Lewes has been the sole assize town for the county.

One doubtful distinction appertains to the Lewes Assizes. In 1735 John Weekes the 'Dumb Man', was sentenced to *peine forte et dure*. This is believed to have been the last occasion on which this punishment was inflicted: the sentence was carried out at Horsham.

During the eighteenth century a number of notorious smugglers were tried at Lewes and in 1831 certain of the 'Captain Swing' rioters were condemned at the assizes. In many southern counties these agricultural rioters were tried by special commissions but at Lewes the normal course of the assize was not apparently interrupted.

The East Sussex Record Office has a brief for the prosecution for the Lewes Lent Assizes of 1855 in an interesting case involving theft from the wreck of a French ship, the *André*, driven on

St Anne's House, Lewes

shore at Seaford. The case contains an implication of 'wrecking'
activities and is, no doubt, typical of many such which must
have been heard at Lewes.

Many sensational murder trials have been heard at Lewes in
recent years for example the 'Brighton Trunk Murders' and
Thorne, Mahon and Haigh.

The judge has a charming house—St Annes House—a little
way from the centre of the town with a delightful view over the
Downs.

For the future the proposal is that in Lewes there should be a
Crown Court served by High Court and Circuit judges until
courts are available at Crawley.

CHAPTER V

The Midland Circuit

O N T H E Midland Circuit the assizes were held in eleven
towns—

Bedford
Aylesbury
Derby
Huntingdon
Leicester
Lincoln
Northampton
Nottingham
Oakham
Birmingham
Warwick

BEDFORD

The town of Bedford spreads out on both sides of the River Ouse.
In the county, the most distinguished house, I suppose, is
Woburn Abbey belonging to the Duke of Bedford. It was
formerly a Cistercian abbey and was granted at the Reformation by Henry VIII to the family of Russell. The fourth Duke
built the present house. I was interested to visit the house and
to see what was provided for the interest and entertainment of
the public who pay for admission. So far as I can see the present
Duke and the Marquess of Bath vie with each other in seeking to
provide bigger and better attractions, including, of course,
wild animals for their visitors.

One of the Russell family, Mr Victor Russell, a twin brother
of Lord Ampthill, was Recorder of Bedford for twenty-two
years. His practice as a barrister lay mostly in the Divorce
Division and his experience of the criminal law was limited;
none the less he held this Recordship for all that time. He

Woburn Abbey

told me how, when he reached the age of 80, he had a letter from the Lord Chancellor of the day suggesting that perhaps the time had come for him to retire. He was much wounded by this and replied saying so, and adding

'I have been Recorder of Bedford for twenty-two years and I really did think I was beginning to get a little better.'

This charming friend died at the age of 91; an example of the truth of the saying which, as the years go by, I quote more and more frequently—

70 young; 80 middle-aged; 90 distinguished.

At the assizes, the judges used to have a Service guard of honour paraded for inspection. It was earlier usually from the R.A.F. at Cardington nearby, where the vast airship sheds are still to be seen. On my last visit however, the parade was provided by Police cadets of both sexes.

The judge's lodgings have changed from time to time. I was lucky enough to stay at Howard House, the house of an old friend, Major Humphrey Whitbread, who travelled all the way from London to dine with me in his own dining-room. Latterly the lodgings have been at Elstow Lodge.

Elstow Lodge, Bedford

It was here that the official Rolls-Royce emerging from the gate of the Lodgings ran into a passing car. Since two police patrol motor cyclists were immediately outside the gate, the accident caused some indignation, and rightly so.

For the future the proposal is that in Bedford there will be magistrates' courts only.

AYLESBURY

The first mention of Aylesbury is in the year 571: the Saxons called it Aeglesburgh ('Church fortified place') and thus the name remains much the same today. In the eighteenth century a house called Prebendal House was, for a time, the home of John Wilkes who was Member of Parliament for Aylesbury from 1757 to 1765 when he was expelled for libel and insolence to the King and Parliament. The County Hall was built in 1720 and housed the Assize Court and the County Council Chamber. Unhappily, this building was recently severely damaged by fire. It was, I believe, a case of arson and

The County Hall, Aylesbury

the court was entirely gutted, together with the Council Chamber. The Crown Court one is glad to know, has been well restored to its original form.

Large tracts of Buckinghamshire were heavily wooded and the Chilterns in particular remained afforested for many years after James I pursued a scheme of disforestation. The hills consequently were much frequented by robbers as well as wild animals. At an early date there was instituted the office of Steward of the Chiltern Hundreds whose task it was to ensure the peaceable passage of the King's subjects. It was then far from the sinecure which it has now become. It was the Place Act of 1742 which established the custom of appointing a resigning Member of Parliament to the Stewardship.

It is of interest to observe that Aylesbury's famous duck breeding industry was established towards the end of the eighteenth century—but whatever the menus say, as a local industry, duck breeding has now completely disappeared.

The old gaol, which dated from mediaeval times (repairs to it were approved in 1189) was immediately behind the County Hall but it was demolished in 1847 and the site used upon which to build the judge's lodgings—and which are also used as a Magistrates' and County Councillors' Club when the judge is not in residence. The judge can reach the ante-room to his court by a first floor passage leading from the lodgings.

Mr Elliott Viney who was High Sheriff of Buckinghamshire in 1964 has most kindly presented me with a copy of his book *The Sheriffs of Buckinghamshire from the 11th Century to the present day.* It contains an admirable description of the Office of High Sheriff. He quotes Dalton in 1687—

> The Office of a Sheriff consisted chiefly in the execution and serving of writs and process of Law to compel men to appear to answer the Law, and also for the taking of men's bodies or lands, according to judgements given in superior courts; and to do this he is the immediate Officer of the King and all His Courts: and he is sworn that he shall truly do this and he must do this without any favour dread or corruption.

Further as times changed Professor Stenton wrote—

> His duties may be mainly formal his authority closely restricted but he still remains a living argument for the continuity of English History.

The Parish Church, Aylesbury

Since the coming of the railways, there has been much loss of pomp and ceremony attending the arrival of the judge of assize in the county and G. H. Fowler in *Recollections of Old County Life* writes—

> In my youth the High Sheriff met the judges about a mile out of the town in a handsome coach, driven by a bewigged coachman and four horses, the coachmen and footmen in handsome liveries, and the Sheriff's javelin men, also in livery, numbering about twenty-four. There was an old custom at Aylesbury that a man, whose office was hereditary, carried a truss of wheaten straw and placed it between the judge's carriage and that of the High Sheriff, that the judge might step on it on leaving the one and entering the other. The man was paid five shillings for the service, and it has been considered by some antiquarians to arise from the ancient Charter of William the Conqueror to Aylesbury, requiring that the town should furnish the King, should he pass that way, with 'three eels for his table, and straw for his chamber in the winter, and green rushes in the summer, and three green geese for his table.'

When I hear of coaches and four I think of the case heard by Mr Justice Darling, who could never resist a pun, in which such a coach had run down a pedestrian. Counsel informed the Court that the coach was lit by acetylene lamps, and said Mr Justice Darling, 'drawn I suppose by a "set o' lean" horses.'

In 1964 in a specially constructed court in the Council Chamber of the Aylesbury Rural District Council was held the trial arising from what is commonly, but perhaps unfortunately, called the *great* train robbery. This trial was presided over by Mr Justice Edmund Davies (now Lord Justice Edmund Davies); there were thirteen accused in the main trial: this part of the case lasted fifty-nine days and the judge's summing up, if I may say so a masterpiece of clarity, took five days. The principal offenders were sentenced to thirty years, a sentence which has given rise to considerable controversy.

For the future the proposal is that in Aylesbury there shall be a Crown Court served by Circuit judges only.

DERBY

In 1954 Derby celebrated the anniversary of the grants of two Charters, the first by Henry II in 1154, the second by Queen Mary in 1554. In the earlier Charter the King said:

County Hall, Derby (1660) and the Judges' Lôdgings

'I rejoice that the burgesses of Derby shall have their laws and customs, as well as they best had them in the time of Henry my grandfather, and William my great grandfather.'

In 1446 another Charter granted to Derby the right to appoint a recorder of the borough who, with the two bailiffs, formed a Commission of the Peace to preside over a Court of Record. The Court of Record was formally held, until the recent changes, and the office of Recorder was known as that of Recorder and Judge of the Borough Court of Record.

The burgesses were empowered to hold the assizes at Derby alternately with Nottingham and it is recorded that the status of the town was raised by the visits of the judge with his train (the 'train' I imagine has been much reduced in size since then) and of the county gentry. (This aspect has much changed since the abolition of Grand Juries in 1933.) This continued until 1569 when Derby received its separate High Sheriff and assizes.

In 1328 the Sheriff was ordered to provide suitable accommodation for the judge of assize and this date marks the origin of the County Hall in St Mary's Gate. The present County Hall has housed the assize courts up to now and was built in 1660 and is thought to be the setting of the trial of Hetty Sorrel in George Eliot's *Adam Bede*.

Perhaps one of the most notable events connected with the Derby assizes was the preaching of an assize sermon at All Saints Church by Dr Henry Sacheverell on the 15 August 1709. Dr. Sacheverell was a Demy at Magdalen College, Oxford, from 1674 to 1724 and a Fellow from 1701 to 1713. He was a friend there of Joseph Addison whose walk by the Cherwell is well known not only to Magdalen men. This cleric preached a similar sermon at St Paul's Cathedral on the 5 November 1709. Both sermons were a fierce indictment of the Whig ministry, asserting that the Church was in danger owing to Government's neglect to guard over its interests. The sermons were printed—the Derby one being dedicated to a kinsman who was High Sheriff of the county. At the time, adherents of the Whigs and those of the Tories were hotly divided. Dr Sacheverell's vehement onslaught on the Government on behalf of the Church which supplied most of the followers of the Tories made him their idol. The Whig minority, although divided about it, decided that Dr Sacheverell should be prosecuted. He was impeached before the House of Lords and charged with 'high crimes and misdemeanours'. The trial lasted from the 27 February to the 23 March 1710 and, after conviction, the sentence was merely suspension from the pulpit for three years —and that the sermons be burned at the Royal Exchange. This made the Defendant a martyr in the eye of the populace and the Government could not resist a general election. The outcome was the return of a great majority of Tories and High Churchmen. The comment has been made:

'The whole policy of the nation and indirectly of the Continent of Europe being changed by the violent rhetoric of a single sermon in the pulpit of All Saints'.

In 1827 it was decided to rebuild County Hall so as to serve the dual purpose of a Court of Justice and of a hall suitable for festivals, balls, dinners and other entertainments. During the assizes little decorum was observed for a description of the hall in that year shows that it resembled a fair—women moving among the throngs vending cakes, fruit and other edibles and thieves occasionally practising their craft under the eye of the judge. In 1814, for example, a man caught in the act of picking the pocket of a countryman in the County Hall while a case was being tried, was sentenced to fourteen years transportation.

In 1817 at a time when the Government feared association

among workmen and threats of unrest, cases of rioting were treated as cases of high treason against the Crown. In June of that year a number of men at Pentrich armed themselves and proceeded to levy blackmail at the houses of the gentry. A man-servant offering resistance was shot dead by the ringleader of the rioters, one Brandreth 'the Nottingham Captain'. The chief rioters were captured by the Yeomanry and brought to Derby where a special Commission of assize was opened with all the ceremony of a State trial. The ring leaders were all sentenced to be hanged and afterwards beheaded. The masked executioner in the performance of his awful task would hold up the head and say

'Behold the head of the traitor Jeremiah Brandreth.'

If the Mayor of Derby calls upon the judge of assize and wears his chain of office, it will be found that the chain, consisting of the capital letter S alternating with interlaced knots of tasselled cords, and in front between two portcullises a Tudor rose, seems strangely familiar. It is, in fact, a collar worn by the Chief Justices of the Queen's Bench and was made for Lord Tenterden in 1818 when he succeeded Lord Ellenborough whose family retained the original chain used by him and his predecessors.

Lord Tenterden was succeeded by Sir Thomas Denman, who, on retiring in 1850, also retained the chain and later sold it to the Corporation. It was Lord Tenterden who, when the reconstructed County Hall was opened for the business of the Summer assizes on the 11 August 1829, congratulated Derby upon the excellence of the building and was pleased to observe that 'in the courts of Lincoln, which are in many respects the best in the Kingdom, the echo is intolerable and occasions great inconvenience' and he was much gratified in finding so very detrimental an effect happily obviated in this court.

The judge's lodgings adjoin the courts and there is here a good example of the occasional usefulness of the Judges' Book in which suggestions are made. From 1908 until 1914 there was a repeated plea for a bathroom. In 1931 it was suggested that a telephone should be installed instead of the judge having to make his way to the police station and use the telephone there. It was installed in 1933. Later a wireless set and a refrigerator were provided, after requests.

I visited Derby in the Autumn of 1963 and was fortunate to

Kedleston Hall, near Derby

be with Lord Justice Diplock as he then was. To be with a member of the Court of Appeal is as unusual as it is helpful. We were followed in Derby by another member of the Court of Appeal, Lord Justice Sellers, who arrived while Lord Justice Diplock was still there and he wrote in the book—

'Diplock and I were here together on Sunday and it is improbable that two judges of the Court of Appeal have been together on circuit in this century, if on any occasion.'

On one Saturday I greatly enjoyed seeing Kedleston Hall when Lord and Lady Scarsdale kindly entertained me and showed me what is really a Curzon museum which particularly interested me with its mementoes of his time as Viceroy of India.

One recalls the story that unlike 'Dining at Blenheim twice a week' the great man and his wife were invited to a small village party and, consulting their diaries, his Lordship said:

'This function, my dear, is I believe what the lower orders refer to as a beano'

but he pronounced it as if on the Continent *béano*.

It was I think in Derby that I tried an old 'lag' for what used to be called 'receiving stolen property'. He had been found in possession of a recently stolen diamond ring and had given an account of how he came to have it which scarcely had the merit of originality—

'I met a seafaring man in a pub—I can't remember the name of the pub. I do not know the sailor's name except that he told me to call him Bill. He said that he had been left the ring by his old aunt and would I like to buy it for 30/-. I looked at it and said, no. Well, he said how about 20/-. No. I'll take 12/6*d*. Done, I said.'

The accused was then cross-examined by counsel for the Crown, whose purpose was to show that such was the obvious value of the ring that 12/6*d* was an absurd price and must have indicated that the transaction was indeed, a dubious one.

'I put it to you', said counsel with that rapier-like thrust for which he was not very famous 'that so ridiculous a price must have lead you to believe that the ring was stolen property.'

The accused denied any such thing but after a little while turned to me confidentially and said—

'Your Worship (they are discerning persons these receivers), when the seaman reduced the price for the third time I must be frank and say that I did feel just a teeny weeny bit superstitious.'

For the future the proposal is that in Derby there should be a Crown Court served by Circuit Judges only.

HUNTINGDON

Huntingdonshire and the Soke of Peterborough now march together as a county and the town of Huntingdon is combined for administrative purposes with Godmanchester. The earliest roll in the county recording the business of the courts of the justices in Eyre is dated 1227. The Circuits established by Edward I, and the assizes on those Circuits, continued as such until the Judicature Act of 1875. By an Order in Council made under that Act, Huntingdon became part of the new South-Eastern Circuit which was made up of the old Home and Norfolk Circuits.

Oliver Cromwell was born in Huntingdon and his family at one time lived at Hinchingbrooke House, later the home of the Earl of Sandwich. Under Cromwell's influence the district became strongly non-Conformist and, in the seventeenth century, many people suffered under the Law for refusing, for conscience sake, to attend religious services in which they did not believe, and for seeking to uphold the right to worship with others of like sympathies, in spite of the illegality of doing so. The assize records of those times are full of presentments by Constables and Grand Juries of the refusals to attend divine service in the parish church on Sunday, or for suffering private meetings of 'supposed Baptists' or Quakers or Popish recusants.

The records include examples of early criminal investigation and detection methods. For example, in 1674 the 'footens' of a felon were tracked to his house where were found shoes which fitted into the tracks in the ploughed field.

Murders were as common then as they are now, but perverse verdicts were sometimes pronounced. In 1668 a jury of sixteen men in the case of the death of Anne Miller, wife of Joseph Miller, said:

'We, the jury, find that Anne Miller, wife of the said Joseph Miller, was sicke about a fortnight before she went out in the night, as before mentioned, and at that time not fully recovered so that we conceive the extreme cold might

Procession at Huntingdon including Mr John Goodliff (High Sheriff) and
William Armstrong (marshal)

The Town Hall, Huntingdon

Paxton Hill House, near Huntingdon

be some cause of her death, and that the ill-usage of her husband might be some other cause thereof.'

The husband had been indicted for battering his wife to death.

The assize court has hitherto been held in the Town Hall, an elegant building erected in 1745 and incorporating a seventeenth-century staircase from an older building.

The judges have been housed in various places. At one time they were housed at the home of Samuel Pepys at Brampton. Pepys was befriended by a relative, the first Lord Sandwich, and was in early days educated at the Grammar School in Huntingdon and lived at a farmhouse belonging to his father at Brampton. It is believed, too, that the judge for a time occupied the Dower House at Hinchingbrooke.

When I visited Huntingdon I stayed at a very agreeable house in the country, Paxton Hill House near St Neots.

It was a special pleasure to me on this occasion to meet the Lord Lieutenant of the County, Lord Hemingford, whose father was Deputy Speaker when I was in the House of Commons.

For the future the proposal is that in Huntingdon there will be magistrates' courts only.

LEICESTER

Hitherto at Leicester one of the assize courts has been held in the Castle so that the history of the Castle is of special interest. It is probable that the first castle was built by William the Conqueror on his progress through the Midlands in 1068. This castle, however, was destroyed in the rebellion against Henry I. The brick front of the present building dates from about 1690 but the hall of the Norman castle remains behind it. It now houses two courts. As Mr Jack Simmons has written—

> The remains of Leicester are thus substantial, and, when you consider the history that lies behind it, the building of the Castle itself soon after the Norman Conquest, the splendour of its life under the Earls and Dukes of Lancaster in the 13th and 14th centuries, the Parliaments that were held here in the reigns of Henry V and Henry VI, the continuing use of the great hall for the Leicestershire Assizes and Quarter Sessions, you realise that here is one the great historical monuments of the Midlands.

Another building of special interest is the Guildhall where the Lord Mayor greets the judge of assize on the opening day of the

The Gatehouse, the Castle, Leicester

The Guildhall, Leicester

sittings. It was originally the hall of the Corpus Christi Gild which was founded in 1343. Many of the leading townsmen belonged to the Gild and in 1495 the Town Council was already meeting in its hall. In 1563 the town bought the hall outright and it was used as the Town Hall until 1876 when the present Town Hall was brought into use.

When I first visited Leicester, the judges' lodgings were in the County Rooms, a rather distinguished but somewhat gloomy building which had been intended for use as an hotel, but was never so used. In recent years, however, the lodgings have been at a charming house close to the Castle, which was arranged and decorated after advice, I believe from some of the Elwes family, the late Mr Justice Elwes having been Recorder of Leicester. The house contains an upstairs sitting-room for the senior judge which is immediately above the gateway to the Castle and was part of the Gatehouse itself.

On my last visit it was of special interest to find that Mr Edmund Brudenell was High Sheriff. He married a daughter of an old friend, Lord Dilhorne. It was delightful to visit Deene Park, a most beautiful house.

In Joan Wake's *The Brudenells of Deene* one reads that before being elected a serjeant-at-law, then the highest rank of the legal profession below that of a judge, Robert Brudenell had, with other contenders, to give two public lectures. The second he delivered in 1501 in the hall of the Inner Temple before a large, distinguished and critical audience. The lecture was approved and he was created a serjeant-at-law or, as it was sometimes called, a serjeant of the coif. Ceremonies of great magnificence followed including a great banquet at Lambeth Palace given by the serjeants and honoured by the presence of the King.

Since the decline of legal business in the County of Rutland, it has been customary for the judge to travel from Leicester to Oakham in order to open the Commission. Critics of the old system condemned this as a waste of time, but I wonder if it was materially so. I describe my visit to Oakham later.

For the future the proposal is that in Leicester there should be a Crown Court served by High Court and Circuit judges.

Lincoln Cathedral

LINCOLN

The name Lincoln comes from the Celtic description of the early British settlement, which is 'Hill Fort by the Pool'. Lincoln Castle was built by William I in 1086. Henry II was crowned there, as was King Stephen.

The Castle was from earliest times the county gaol, the shire court sat in the Shire Hall and the judges on circuit held their courts there. In 1826 the Shire Hall and Assize Courts were rebuilt and in 1831 the Castle was bought by the Lincolnshire County Justices from the Duchy of Lancaster—the price being £2,000.

By an Act of Parliament of 1809 the justices for the three divisions of the County—Lindsey, Kesteven and Holland—were enabled to provide a house for the judges of assize. This house was also built about 1826 just outside the castle gate and but a short distance from the Cathedral.

Executions used to take place on the roof of Cobb Hall, the small tower at the right-hand side of the entrance to the Castle.

They were at first public occasions and indeed children were taken to watch them as a lesson in the need for uprightness. In 1812 the Magistrates ordered an execution to take place between the two gates with a strong escort of constables owing to the rumours of a possible rescue.

When executions ceased to be in public the gallows were erected on the corner of the assize court where the entrance to the cells now is.

In *Hanging in Chains* by Albert Hartshorne there is this passage—

> In 1808 Thomas Otter was hanged at Lincoln for murdering his paramour. Afterwards he was hung in chains at 'Gibbet Lane' Saxilby. Later some tomtits built their nest in his skull and reared several young ones. A local poet composed these macabre lines in the form of a riddle:
>
> > '10 tongues in one head
> > 9 living and one dead
> > One flew forth to fetch some bread
> > To feed the living in the dead'
>
> The answer is 'The tomtit that built
> > in Tommy Otter's Head'.

The assize court photograph at Lincoln, including Captain H. N. Nevile (Sheriff)

The Lodgings, Lincoln

The Courts, the Castle, Lincoln

Lord and Lady Diplock and David Darbyshire (marshal) at Lincoln

The cathedral is said to be the earliest purely Gothic building in Europe. Plans for the great church were adapted from those of Rouen in about 1086 and the building was consecrated a few years later. Lincoln, the enormous diocese which in early times extended from the Thames to the Humber, was one of the thirteen cathedrals of the old foundation served by secular canons. On my last visit I spent a long time looking for the famous imp and fortunately met the Dean who pointed it out to me high up in the carved capital of one of the columns.

The city of Lincoln is itself a county and so has a City Sheriff.

In March 1852 there was a remarkable scene in the assize court when Mr Justice Maule was presiding at a murder trial. The local newspaper heading was 'Extraordinary and Eccentric Conduct of a Judge'. It appears that the judge complaining of lack of ventilation ordered that the windows of the court be opened. There was some delay at which the judge threatened to have 'the windows broken' if his order was not instantly carried out. Two or three minutes passed and the judge losing all patience ordered the windows to be smashed, a bailiff's wand having been handed up to a grand juror for that purpose. The glass was smashed and tumbled on the heads of the people below eliciting peals of laughter from the members of the Bar and the whole court. At this the judge said

'Those gentlemen who wish to indulge in such indecorous behaviour must go and indulge themselves out of court.'

On my first visit to Lincoln the senior judge was Lord Justice Diplock, then a member of the Court of Appeal now a Lord of Appeal in Ordinary. He was pleased I think to come on circuit again and happily it was during the hunting season so that his horse box joined the judicial progression to the lodgings and from then on to a nearby stable. Sir Kenneth Diplock would always have a day's hunting if it were possible. He called his horse 'Circuit'. Thus if an enquiry came as to the whereabouts of his Lordship, the answer was wholly accurate:

'Away on Circuit.'

For the future the proposal is that in Lincoln there shall be a High Court and Crown Court served by High Court and Circuit judges.

NORTHAMPTON

In Northampton the assize court is a very beautiful one with a

The Courts and Lodgings, Northampton

specially attractive ceiling. In the ceiling, there is a face over the Grand Jury gallery. If, from the gallery, the fishing-rod device used for lowering the bills of indictment to the Clerk of Assize touches this face, its tongue moves in and out on a hinge.

The Coat of Arms behind the judge's chair is of the time of Charles II.

The judges have as their lodgings a house adjoining the courts.

Mr Maurice Healey often appeared in the courts at Northampton and, I think, lived nearby. He was a connoisseur of wine—did he not write a book on claret? The story goes that, having travelled from Northampton to Bristol, he paid a call at the cellars of Messrs Avery and there saw the senior partner. He said—and alas one cannot reproduce the soft Irish burr—

'Mr Avery I see from your list that you have a sherry priced at 3/6d a bottle—are ye able to recommend it?'

Mr Avery replied—

'Mr Healey, I am assured that it helps to make a quite excellent trifle.'

to which the reply came

'Mr Avery, ye are an honest wine merchant. I will deal with ye.'

This always greatly amused my friend the late Mr Ernest Atkinson, London Editor of the *Birmingham Post*, and his wife Margaret, both of them having written much about wines.

For the future the proposal is that in Northampton there should be a Crown Court served by High Court and Circuit judges.

NOTTINGHAM

In 1068 William the Conqueror ordered the building of a castle at Nottingham and by 1131 it had become a stone building—no doubt originally it was built of wood. The Castle was a Royal house for over 500 years. Dr Robert Thoroton in 1677 wrote:

> Neither is there any place anything near so far distant from London that I know of in all England, which hath so often given entertainment and residence to the Kings and Queens of this Realm since the Norman Conquest.

In 1284 a Charter of Edward I granted the right to choose a mayor and two bailiffs. This Charter also granted leave to hold a fifteen days' fair in addition to the already established eight days fair which was the celebrated Goose Fair. Of this the late Sir Arthur Ward has written—

> The Old Goose Fair was one of the annual outlets of the wild ones, but in deference to the locals one must remember the great influx from all the surrounding districts and towns. The Goose Fair in those days (about 100 years ago) was held in the old Market Place ordinarily fitted with bright stalls from which one could purchase almost anything required for the household, but all cleared away to make space for the caravans, swings, roundabouts, shows, ginger-bread crackers, ice-cream, ginger-pop, multicoloured mineral stalls, all lighted by hissing flaring paraffin lamps. At night many thousands made merry while the hundreds of pocket pickers indulged their nefarious practices.

The old castle was eventually destroyed by order of Parliament and a mansion house was built on the same site, the owner being the Duke of Newcastle.

The City of Nottingham is also a county so that again the judges are greeted by two Sheriffs and their Under Sheriffs, as well as the Lord Mayor who is good enough to call upon the

The Guildhall, Nottingham

judges on the first day of the sittings. The two Commissions hitherto have been read in the Guildhall and in the Shirehall, or, as it was anciently called, the King's Hall. It was in 1448 that King Henry VI gave a Charter to the town which was to be separated from the county, but the King excepted from the City (then made a county itself) 'our Castle of Nottingham and our Messuage called the King's Hall wherein is our Gaol for our counties of Nottingham and Derby.'

It is said that the assizes began to be held in the county in 1194 in the reign of Richard I.

Sir Arthur Ward further recalls some of the historical events concerned with the assizes. On 20 March 1724, according to the *Nottingham Courant*

the judge (Mr Justice Powis) had gone into the County Hall and a great crowd of people being there, a tracing or two that supported the floor broke and fell in, and several people fell in with it, about three yards down into the cellar underneath. This caused great consternation in court, some apprehending that the Hall might fall, others crying 'fire' which made several people climb out of the windows. The judge also being terribly frightened cried

The Park, Nottingham

out—A plot, a plot! But the consternation was soon over and the court proceeded to business. However, the judge told the Grand Jury that he would lay a fine on the county of £2,000 for not providing a better Hall, not doubting that if they built a new one, or got the old one well repaired, that on their petition His Majesty would remit the fine. At the request of the foreman of the Grand July the fine was suspended.

The county, however, successfully disputed the judge's power to impose the fine.

None the less, in 1768 it was decided to build a new hall on the old site and to be deemed within the county. It thus constitutes a separate parish, possibly the smallest in England, the sole inhabitants being the caretaker and his wife.

At Nottingham the assize judges, often three of them, occupy a commodious house in the Park surrounded by very large houses, no doubt the residences of Nottingham's prosperous lace makers and other merchant princes towards the end of the nineteenth century. The Park was at one time the property of the University of Oxford.

It was on the way to Nottingham by train on one occasion that two travellers in the restaurant car were heard talking together. It was quite soon after a specially appointed tribunal under the distinguished chairmanship of Mr Justice Lynskey had finished its enquiries into the alleged malpractices of a man who was said to have bribed a junior Minister of the Crown. One traveller said to his companion:

'By the way, did you ever hear what happened to that rogue Lynskey? Is he still in prison?'

This good example of failure to read the news with care was often referred to with glee by Mr Justice Lynskey himself.

For the future the proposal is that in Nottingham there should be a High Court and a Crown Court served by High Court and Circuit judges.

OAKHAM

Oakham is a small country town in the smallest county in England and, at the assizes held there, the volume of business must have been smaller than at any others in the Kingdom. The town is said to take its name from the magnificent oak trees in

The Castle, Oakham

the neighbourhood. Its history goes back to Saxon times and it appears in the Domesday Book.

Edward the Confessor gave Rutland to his Queen Edith and by his will directed that, after Queen Edith's death, Rutland should go to the Abbey of Westminster. The tithes and church of Oakham and part of the Manor, now known as Deanshold, were eventually given to the Abbot.

The pride of Oakham is, naturally enough, the castle. It is likely that it was built by Walkelin, the son of Henry de Ferrers, between 1180 and 1190, and was built originally as a fortified manor house. The castle has been described as the most perfect specimen of domestic architecture of the twelfth century which exists in any country. In many accounts the castle is referred to as a Hall.

In the Hall, a unique feature is the collection of horseshoes. Custom requires:

> that the first time any Peer of this Kingdom shall pass through the precincts of this Lordship, he shall forfeit as a homage, a shoe from the horse whereon he rideth, unless he redeem it with money.

The oldest horseshoe dates from the reign of Queen Elizabeth I and one of the most recent is that of Queen Elizabeth II presented in May 1967. The collection had reached well over 200 when last counted, and it is to be noted that the rank of the Peer, whose horseshoe it is, is shown by the form of the coronet which surmounts the shoe.

This means of levying a toll is similar to that which was adopted at one time by a Mayor of Dover who required ½d. for every horse passing through the town, the money going towards the repair of the harbour.

It recalls to my mind the old mathematical story of the blacksmith who was asked by the passing, and plainly wealthy, traveller how much he required for shoeing his horse. The traveller thought it highly reasonable when the blacksmith said all he would accept would be ¼d. for the first nail, ½d., for the second, 1d. for the third, 2d. for the fourth, and so on, doubling until all 28 nails were paid for. I used to think it would add up to about £25; it works out at well over £250,000.

It has been in the Hall that the assizes since 1375 have been held, the last being held in June 1970. I was fortunate enough to open the Commission at Oakham in the Summer of 1966. I was then in the lodgings at Leicester and drove over quite early on a misty morning. I well remember finding the High Sheriff and Under Sheriff awaiting me at the county boundary; they both wore black top hats and stood on the verge by the side of the road, looking to my mind irresistibly as if waiting for the arrival of the other side to take part in a pending duel. Having changed into the Rutland car, we drove to a private house in Oakham, where I robed, and we then proceeded to the church and to the Castle where the Commission was opened. The High Sheriff kindly gave me a sherry party and I was back in Leicester sitting there at 2 p.m. In my opinion interest and preserved tradition warranted the loss of half a day's judicial time.

The Urban District Council of Oakham perpetuates the names of three of its local characters as of special historical interest.

First, Jeffry Hudson

> the least man of the least County in England, who figures in Scott's *Peveril of the Peak* was born in Oakham in 1619. At the age of 9, when only 18″ high, he was taken into the Buckingham household at Burley. He was served up to Queen Henrietta in a pie, later becoming her page. He was knighted and had many adventures overseas being twice captured by pirates.

Second, Titus Oates, originator of the Popish plot, was born in Oakham in 1649, the son of a teacher.

Third, Sir Edward Digby, one of Guy Fawkes' fellow conspirators, who had an estate nearby. There is a tradition, which cannot be verified, that the Gunpowder Plot was hatched in a room over the north porch of the village church at Stoke Dory. DRY

For the future the proposal is that in Oakham there should be magistrates' courts only.

BIRMINGHAM

The derivation of the name Birmingham is obscure and about 150 different spellings have been noted. Although described as 'fanciful etymology', I like the historian Hutton's theory that the name comes from three words—BROM (Broom) WYCH (a descent) and HAM (a home), making together 'the home on the hill by the heath'.

Modern historians in Birmingham are, I think, too modest about the antiquity of the place. In 1166 Henry II granted a Market Charter to Peter de Bermingham, the Lord of the Manor, but it would seem to have been proved that the place was in existence as a community in Saxon times. This proof came in 1309 when one William de Bermingham, in a law suit, showed that his ancestors had a market there and levied tolls before the Conquest. The fortunes of the family declined sharply in 1527 when Edward de Bermingham was deprived of his property by John Dudley, Duke of Northumberland, who, it is said, trumped up a charge of riot and robbery against him and procured Birmingham for himself. On the attainder of Dudley, however, the Manor passed to the Crown.

At the time of the Civil War the citizens of Birmingham sided with the Parliamentarians and indeed in 1642, when Charles was marching from Shrewsbury to relieve Banbury, the Birmingham people seized much of his baggage, including plate, money and wine which they sent to the Parliamentary garrison at Warwick. Further they supplied many thousands of sword blades to the Parliamentary forces, but declined 'With a peremptory malice for His Majesty', to supply Royalist troops, a fact which was not forgotten when Prince Rupert attacked the town in 1643.

By 1700 the city's reputation as a great industrial centre had begun and steps were taken to remove the prejudices against 'Brummagem Ware'.

It has been said that, in the middle of the nineteenth century Birmingham badly needed a local leader and in 1869 he appeared in the person of Joseph Chamberlain. In that year he was elected to the Council and made Mayor in 1873, being twice re-elected to that office. Under his guidance the town was raised to a place of great prominence.

In about 1935 my family entertained Sir Austen Chamberlain when he came to speak in Chester, at a meeting at which I took the chair. He was a charming guest and three things stand out in my recollection of his visit. The first was that he told me that he always felt extremely ill and nervous for a considerable time before making a major speech. This was highly consoling to a beginner in politics, coming as it did from a great statesman. The second was that, having been given a private sitting-room in which to cogitate over the affairs of State, he was found in fact to be closely bent over *The Times* cross-word puzzle. The third was that when we all asked to see the Garter which had recently been conferred upon him, and which he was to wear the night after the meeting at the Jewellers' dinner in Birmingham, he found that he had lost the key of the case and it had to be forced open.

In 1839 the town was granted its own Quarter Sessions, Recorder, Clerk of the Peace and Coroner.

It appears from Mr C. A. Vince's *History of the Corporation of Birmingham* that the City had ambitions to become an assize town in 1853 and an application to become such was first made in 1857. Other applications followed and some suggested that an assize district should be formed with Birmingham at the centre. In 1883 the town was granted an assize status. Plans were made for the new courts and on the 23rd March 1887 Queen Victoria laid the foundation stone. This was the Jubilee year of her reign and it was appropriate that, with Her Majesty's permission, the courts were to be called The Victoria Courts. I note in passing that in the Mayor's address of welcome to the Queen he ended by wishing that—

'Your Majesty may long be spared to preside over the destinies of this mighty Empire.'

On the 30th July 1891 the assizes were first held there, the judges being Lord Chief Justice Coleridge and Mr Justice Wills.

Victoria Law Courts, Birmingham

The Judges' Lodgings, Edgbaston, Birmingham

At the back of the Victoria Courts in Steelhouse Lane, is Fountain Court, a newly-built suite of barristers' chambers set around a central court. Its design follows the pattern of the London Inns of Court and it is the first of its kind to be built in the provinces since the fourteenth century.

The judges' lodgings are out at Edgbaston with a delightful view over almost open country to some of the University buildings. The old house on the site was demolished and a new building put up. It is a most comfortable and commodious house but the comment was made that it looked somewhat institutional as if it might be an Old Peoples' Home, to which one of the judges retorted

'Well, that is just about what it is!'

A story of Mr Justice Rigby Swift, and one which is vouched for, is that one day at the Victoria Law Courts he was trying a case in which the plaintiff, a middle-aged widow, was claiming damages for personal injuries, which included injuries to the

Faulks, J., Stable, J. and Mocatta, J. at the Birmingham Lodgings

Judge Lewis McCreery, Dunn, J., Latey, J. at Birmingham Lodgings

eyes, which she said produced double vision. She was represented
by one of Birmingham's most famous, and consequently busiest
members of the Bar, Mr Arthur Ward. While the plaintiff was
in the witness box, Mr Ward's clerk came into court and tugged
his master's gown, showing clearly that he had just come from
the other court with an urgent message. The judge, who missed
nothing, thereupon addressed the plaintiff—

'Do you tell me, madam, that you see two of everything.'

'Yes, my Lord.'

'Oh, do you see two clocks behind me?'

'Yes, my Lord.'

'And do you see two of me?'

'Yes, my Lord.'

'And tell me, do you see two of your learned counsel, Mr,
Arthur Ward?'

'Yes, my Lord.'

'Indeed, that is just as well for one of him is wanted in the
other court.'

For the future the proposal is that in Birmingham there
should be a High Court and a Crown Court served by High
Court and Circuit judges.

WARWICK

Warwick is a beautiful survival of the age of mediaeval walled towns. The Castle stands magnificently—high up above the River Avon—and, what is known as Ethelfleda's Mound, is reputed to be the Keep of the Norman castle begun by William the Conqueror in 1068 and given into the charge of Henry de Beaumont, the first Earl of Warwick, in 1088.

The assize service is held, but a hundred yards or so from the courts, in the Collegiate Church of St Mary, a foundation going back to a date before the Conquest.

Coventry was once an assize town, but, before Birmingham became an assize town, Warwick was the busiest assize town on the Midland Circuit.

The courts are in the County Hall, which is of some age but the interior of which has been re-built. The arched entrance to the offices was the 'death house' of those under sentence of death. There is also to be seen an underground dungeon condemned by John Howard, the great prison reformer. Where the police station now is, used to be the town gaol and Charles Dickens once watched an execution there.

It was at the courts at Warwick that Abraham Thornton was tried. He was acquitted and at once the nearest male relative of the alleged victim demanded a re-trial, according to the law of the times. In reply to this Thornton claimed the right of 'trial by combat'. Soon afterwards these laws as to the right of retrial and trial by combat were repealed.

When I first went to Warwick, the senior judge was the late Mr Justice Winn (later Lord Justice Winn). He had been a most distinguished Naval Officer in the War becoming a Captain, which is unusual for an officer coming straight from civilian life, and was wholly occupied in 'spotting' enemy submarines, which he did with outstanding skill. It is not surprising, therefore, that he brought with him as a marshal, a serving Naval officer, at one time in fact a secretary of the First Sea Lord, Sir Caspar John. Commander Leonard Critchley, whom I mention elsewhere, greatly pleased me by saying to his judge when the car had arrived at the door:

'Boat's alongside, Sir'.

This brings to mind an old friend who unhappily died a

The County Hall, Warwick

few years ago. He was Mr Leo Gradwell who started as a junior
member of the Bar in Liverpool, gave outstanding service as a
Naval officer during the 1939 War taking convoys to the Arctic
and later became a Metropolitan magistrate. In his early days
he had some human weaknesses (haven't we all) but these he
could not help in a witty way exaggerating quite absurdly. A
devout Catholic, he used to say that when he went to confessional
the priest would look out of his box, see him at the head of the
waiting penitents and announce loudly to them:

'Leo is here. No other case will be taken today!'

The judges' lodgings in Warwick are in the County Hall adjoining the courts.

For the future the proposal is that in Warwick there should
be a High Court and a Crown Court until more courts are
available at Birmingham, Coventry and Stoke-on-Trent.

CHAPTER VI

The Northern Circuit

O N T H E Northern Circuit there have been hitherto five
Assize towns—

> Carlisle
> Lancaster
> Liverpool
> Manchester
> Appleby

CARLISLE

In 1958 Carlisle celebrated the 800th anniversary of the grant-
ing of its first Royal Charter and Mr C. R. Hudleston has
compiled a list of Sheriffs, starting with the first Sheriff of
Carlisle (1098–1100) with an initial only 'G' and with the first
Sheriff of Cumberland (1175–1179), Robert de Vaux. It is noticeable how the county names recur. The Curwens have provided
33 Sheriffs; the Musgraves 23; the Lowthers 20; the Lamploughs
and Dacres 14 each; the Lawsons 13 and the Hudlestons and
Senhouses 12 each. In this long list, I notice in 1271 Roger de
Pokelinton and that brings to mind that when I went to the
assizes in 1946—that is nearly 700 years later—Guy Pocklington-
Senhouse was the Sheriff.

The assize court is in the Citadel, built in 1541 at a time
when Henry VIII was in process of strengthening the castle
defences.

The first assizes were held at Carlisle shortly after 1166 and
there are references in the Pipe Rolls to the Justices in Cumberland in the twelfth century.

By a Statute of Henry VI in 1435 it was provided

> that the Sessions of the Justices to take assizes and to deliver gaols
> in the County of Cumberland be holden in time of peace and of

The Citadel, Carlisle

truce in the said City of Carlisle and in none other place within
the same County: as it hath been used and accustomed of old
Time.

The trials at Carlisle following the '45' are of special interest.
In 1745 Carlisle was occupied by the Scots under Prince Charles
Edward Stuart, who invaded England. The Union of England
and Scotland had removed all reasonable necessity for maintain-
ing the fortifications and Carlisle surrendered on the 15 Novem-
ber. On 15 April 1746, the Highlanders were defeated at
Culloden and the Prince became a fugitive. Thereafter, 382
prisoners were brought to Carlisle for trial at the assizes. On
12 August 1746 Chief Baron Parker, Sir Thomas Burnet, Sir
Thomas Dennison and Baron Clark opened the Commission.
There was a Grand Jury of twenty-three persons and one of the
Grand Jurors called for on 12 August 1746 was Humphrey
Senhouse of Netherell. One of those who served on the last
Grand Jury ever to sit in Carlisle, which was in October 1933,
was a descendant, namely Colonel Guy Pocklington-Senhouse
to whom reference has already been made. So large was the
number of prisoners that it was arranged that most of them
should have the option of drawing lots for the selection of one
out of every twenty to stand trial, the other nineteen to submit to

The Lodgings, Carlisle

transportation. In this strangely unorthodox way the numbers to be tried were reduced to 127. They appeared on 9 September 1746, very few were acquitted and those who were convicted were sentenced by Chief Baron Parker on 22 and 23 September 1746. Ninety-six were sentenced to death of whom thirty-one were executed. It is recorded that for this horrifying task the executioner, one William Stout of Hexham, received a fee of 20 guineas and perquisites of the victims' clothing and belongings.

The judge's lodgings in recent years have been an attractive house a little way out of the town to the North and once the home of a distinguished Under Sheriff, Mr Lionel Lightfoot.

Carlisle was a popular circuit town and I have been there many times with no work, and no hope of any. The circuit always entertained the assize judge to dinner at the County Hotel by the railway station and often, on these occasions, a most senior Silk presided. He was Mr Edward Wooll, Q.C., a playwright and a wit, as well as a notably distinguished member of the Bar. He was also Recorder of Carlisle for many years, steadfastly refusing to retire even when he reached the late eighties. Presiding when the judges were guests of the Bar mess, he would often begin his speech like this:—

There are judges AND judges. Our guests this evening fall into the latter category.

Was this a compliment or was it not?

From Carlisle it was easy indeed to reach the beauties of the Lake District, so much beloved by Mr Justice Norman Birkett, later Lord Birkett of Ulverston, taking the territorial part of his title from his childhood home. Just before he died he made an eloquent appeal in the House of Lords to save the beauties of the Lake District.

Lord Birkett had a mellifluous voice, a gift of clear and attractive expression and a considerable wit. He was too one of the few people I have known who, I believe, really enjoyed making after-dinner speeches.

In court it was always agreeable to appear before him.

When he was in the Court of Appeal I was against an old friend, Mr Henry Nelson, Q.C., who came of an eminent business family in Liverpool. He was arguing that an award of damages to a client of his for the loss of an eye was too low and was urging upon the Court that the disability of having but one eye was grave indeed and merited much larger damages.

'But, Mr Nelson,' said Lord Justice Birkett, 'your distinguished ancestor seemed to get along very well.'

On another occasion I applied to Mr Justice Birkett that a case should be fixed for a certain date in Liverpool before the judges moved on to Manchester. It was a substantial case and the judge asked:

'Mr Nield, is there time to dispose of that case in Liverpool *ere* we go to Manchester'?

and it was said in such a way that one would have thought that the judges were really on their way to 'Samarkand'.

One last mention of Lord Birkett I must make. I once bought a quite expensive American book on aids to after-dinner speaking. Alas, there was only one passage of any value to me and that came in the shape of a story all the way from England and told by Lord Birkett:

'When I sit down after a difficult argument presented to the Court, I always wonder if I have left anything out,' said leading Counsel.

'When I have completed a complicated operation,' said the distinguished surgeon, 'I always wonder if I have left anything in.'

For the future the proposal is that in Carlisle there should be a High Court and a Crown Court served by High Court and Circuit judges.

LANCASTER

I have often thought that there is a broad resemblance between the grouping of ancient buildings on the top of a hill at Lancaster, and that at Durham. At Lancaster there is the beautiful old parish church where the assize service is held and the magnificent castle, part of which dates from the end of the eleventh century, and, a little lower down the hill, a fine old stone house which is the judges' lodgings.

The setting for the assize courts—the Castle itself—teems with history. A suitable starting point, for the purpose of this record, is, I think, the year 1267 when Henry III gave the county and the Castle to his youngest son Edmund who became the first Earl of Lancaster. After several vicissitudes, the earldom was granted to Henry Plantaganet, and his son was created the first Duke of Lancaster. As such he exercised almost Royal powers, appointing his own courts and his own Sheriff. The Palatinate dukedom fell to John of Gaunt who died in 1399. He was succeeded by Henry of Bolingbroke who, as Henry IV, granted a charter, declaring the lands and possessions of the Duchy of Lancaster separate from those of the Crown, and to be vested in the Chancellor of the Duchy. From then on the Duchy has been Crown lands, so that, in the county, the loyal toast always is 'The Queen, Duke of Lancaster'. This special status of the Duchy is shown in several features. For example magistrates for the county are chosen, not as elsewhere by the Lord High Chancellor of Great Britain, but by the Chancellor of the Duchy, who also recommends persons for appointment to the county court bench. Again the Sovereign appoints the High Sheriff at a ceremony separate from that at which the names of the other sheriffs—except Cornwall, the other Royal Duchy—are pricked.

The assizes have been held in the Castle at Lancaster since about 1166, the year in which justices itinerant were first appointed after the Assize of Clarendon. Quarter Sessions have been held in the Castle since about 1361.

The Lodgings, Lancaster

In the Shire Hall, which was completed in 1798, is a large collection of javelins which were carried by guards attending the judges and High Sheriff. There is also a unique collection of shields bearing the coats of arms of Sovereigns, Constables of the Castle and High Sheriffs, dating from the twelfth century. Every year there is a short ceremony, attended by the judges, at which the shield of the High Sheriff of the day is hung.

It was Mr William Garnett, High Sheriff in 1879, who was responsible for the collection of the shields. His son, Mr W. J. Garnett, was High Sheriff twice—once in 1937 and again in 1941—and he added the banners of the Sheriff's trumpeters.

The Crown Court also dates from 1798. In the dock there is still to be seen the holdfast arm into which the left hand of the unhappy prisoner, ordered to be branded, was thrust, while the red hot brand was pressed against the thumb to produce an 'M', to denote malefactor. This barbarous act took place in the presence of the judge and jury and the brander looking at his work would say to the judge 'a fair mark, my lord'. The last use of the branding iron is believed to have been in 1811. Up to 150 years ago accused persons were required in court to hold up their left hands so that any 'M' might be seen and thus

The Castle, Lancaster

Lord Chief Justice Parker at Lancaster

Lady Parker, the author's sister Beryl and Lord Parker

indicate previous convictions. How different this was from the present system where, almost invariably, the criminal history of the most hardened miscreant is closely hidden from the jury.

On my last assize at Lancaster I was greatly pleased to be with the then Lord Chief Justice, Lord Parker. He and his wife and my sister took pleasure in driving to the close-by Lake District and enjoying its scenery.

For the future the proposal is that in Lancaster there should be a High Court and a Crown Court served by High Court and Circuit judges.

LIVERPOOL

The assize courts are housed in the Parthenon—like St George's Hall which is a fine example of the classical style.

The judges' lodgings are at Newsham House, Newsham Park. This is a distinguished house dating from the end of the eighteenth century and built upon the site of a much older manor house. It was one Thomas Molyneux (not of Lord Sefton's family) who built the present house, but it was bought, with the entire estate, by the Liverpool Corporation in 1846.

Latterly my marshal, David Steel, took me often to the lake to watch the boating. He was an Oxford Rowing Blue.

Earlier, namely in 1823, the Liverpool Corporation had petitioned the Secretary of State to accord to Liverpool the status of an assize town. In consideration of the Government acceding to this request, the Corporation undertook to place the courts at the disposal of the judges and Bar attending the Northern Circuit and also to provide suitable lodgings and accommodation for the judges. The first assize was held in Liverpool on 7 August 1835 and the judges occupied Newsham House in 1868.

Having gone into chambers in Liverpool after being called to the Bar, I hope to be forgiven if I spend rather longer than I would otherwise do when considering this important assize town and if I indulge in reminiscence.

Many notable figures in the Law have come from Liverpool and none more notable than F. E. Smith, the great 'F.E.', who became Lord Chancellor and, at one time, Secretary of State for India. Another great figure, Mr Justice Bigham, when he became a peer, took the title Viscount Mersey, saying

'You see, I must leave the Atlantic for F.E.'

St George's Hall, Liverpool

Newsham House, Liverpool

Dermot Wright (marshal), Nield, J., Cantley, J., Baker, J., Chapman, J. and Mr John Wilson (Under Sheriff) at Newsham House

However, F.E., not renowned for undue modesty, preferred to become the Earl of Birkenhead, his family estate agents' business having been long established in Hamilton Square, Birkenhead.

It is reported that at one time F.E. was asked to name the great milestones in his distinguished career. He said, 'my call to the Bar, my taking Silk, my appointment as Lord Chancellor,' and was about to continue when his wife interposed saying:

'Freddy, what about me?'

to which the great man retorted—

'My dear, they asked about milestones, not millstones!'

He could not resist the riposte, however far it was from the truth.

My father was a solicitor in Liverpool and at one time President of the Liverpool Law Society. His firm, however, was not a litigious one.

I recall making in my first year the sum of £93 which was really rather handsome. My great ambition was to have delivered to me at least one brief a week, and a brief in those days meant one in the police court, as it was then called, marked £1. 3. 6d: £1. 1. 0d. for Counsel and 2/6d. for his clerk. Still, if one is a little pleased with one's achievements, one's true

The author's sister with Lady Lyell, Lyell, J. and Nicholas Beresford-Jones
(marshal) at Newsham House

level is always found. At this time, alas it is 1925, I was Junior of the Circuit and, as such, I was deputed by the members of the Liverpool Bar to buy a quite expensive piece of silver to be presented to the Prosecuting Solicitor, a Mr Bold, upon his retirement. I had been at the assizes watching and, I fear, unemployed, and returned by a narrow alley lined with warehouses from which merchandise was constantly raised and lowered and therefore known to us all as 'Contributory Negligence Lane' carrying my dark blue robe bag over my shoulder. In North John Street I stepped into a well-known silversmiths, looking forward with confidence to making this substantial purchase. The black-coated shop assistant took one look at me and my blue bag advanced and said—

'No old silver today, thank you.'

In those days we dined every night of the assize in the Bar mess at the old London and North Western Hotel. We had two private rooms, an ante-room and a dining-room, an excellent cellar of wine, a fine collection of silver and a dignified butler called Hartley. We dined at 6.30 so that the members could come straight on from their conferences after court and get home reasonably early to prepare for the next day's work. It was a helpful reminder of the time when, punctually every evening at 8.45, Hartley fell from his chair behind the screen where he was stationed to receive our orders. I once, and it was indeed a silly question, asked him what happened to the inch or so of port or sherry left in the decanters on most evenings. His answer was—

'Sir, you may be sure it is not wasted.'

One of the greatest figures on the Northern Circuit was Sir Francis Kyffin-Taylor, later Lord Maenan. He has the distinction of having a building in the Inner Temple named after him —the Kyffin-Taylor Building: a distinction which is shared with an old friend, Mr. Kenneth Carpmael, Q.C., after whom the Carpmael Building in the Middle Temple is named. Sir Francis was the presiding judge of the Liverpool Court of Passage for years and years and years. The court is a local one which will disappear: its jurisdiction is unlimited in amount but confined to causes arising within the boundaries of the City. It takes its name from the passage of shipping and seafaring men through the Port of Liverpool. Many distinguished lawyers would be the first to agree that they learnt much of their advocacy from Sir Francis Kyffin-Taylor: such men as Lord Justice Singleton, Lord Justice

Lord and Lady Kilmuir

Sellers, Mr Justice Lynskey, Mr Justice Pritchard, Sir David Maxwell Fyfe, later the Earl of Kilmuir and Lord Chancellor (he and his wife Sylvia were among my greatest friends), Lord Shawcross, Mr Justice Brabin and others. No doubt Sir Francis had some weaknesses as well as outstanding strength: he nearly always found that the city tram-car had jerked and thrown the plaintiff to the ground and that the City omnibus had stopped before the correct stop and flung the plaintiff down: but as the average damages awarded were about £12.10.0d. or in moments of great generosity £20, few appeals were pursued.

Although, I fear, this section of the record is very much about myself, I feel I must record that in 1948 I was appointed Chancellor of the Diocese of Liverpool. The Bishop, Dr Clifford Martin, sent for me and asked if I would undertake the office. I protested that I had no knowledge of ecclesiastical law, which the Bishop countered by saying

'Well, you can always look it up.'

With this flattering invitation in mind I went to Oxford to his house on Boars Hill to see Judge Challoner Dowdall, who had been Chancellor for many years—he was then in his eighties. He gave me some account of the duties of the office and then this excellent advice—in three words—'beware of images.' In the end, I was honoured to accept the office and to exercise the jurisdiction involving the grant of faculties; as Judge Dowdall said:
'I have granted so many faculties I have very few left.'

Another great figure from the local Bar in Liverpool was Mr Justice Philip Rigby Swift. He was regarded, I think rightly, as a fierce judge and I am glad to be permitted to quote the following verse composed by Sir F. E. Pritchard, who then held the office of Solicitor-General of the Circuit and who was charged with the task of calling attention to the activities of junior counsel in Liverpool. He said, addressing the Junior of the Circuit as the custom is:

Mr. Junior,
I was sitting in the Crown Court on the first day of this Assize, wondering what matters to bring to your attention tonight in connection with the Stuffs on the Northern Circuit, when by pure chance I put my hand under the desk and there discovered a lengthy document which appeared to be in the form of a popular ballad.

The author is unknown to me although I rather suspect *Macaulay* (Ian Macaulay was then Clerk of Assize), but as the ballad is a narrative relating to the very recent activities of some of the Stuffs, I decided to adopt it as my speech, and, with your permission, I now propose to read it to you. It runs as follows:—

Sir Philip Swift of Liverpool
By his black cap he swore
That the Great Northern Circuit
Should live in peace no more
By his black cap he swore it
And nam'd Commission Day
And bade *Bill Graham* give it forth
That he was shortly coming north
And with Macnaghten J.

To Cumberland and Lancashire
Bill Graham spread the word
And ev'ryone who lov'd his loins
His loins began to gird

Shame on the coward who shivers
    And curses on the MOME
When Rigby Swift of Liverpool
    Leaves London and comes home.

But by the yellow Mersey
    Was tumult and affright
And *Baucher* went a nasty green
    Whilst *Howard Jones* turn'd white
And all around the City
    The Stuffs stopp'd up the ways
Discussing what might be their fate
    Before a few more days.

They held a meeting standing
    Outside St George's Hall
Short time was there, you well may guess,
    For making plans at all—
Out spake *O. G. Morris* roundly
    Will naught allay your fears?
His bite is nothing to his bark,
    I've known the man for years.

Just then *McNeile* came flying
    All white with haste and fear
'To arms! To arms! You men,' he cried,
    'Sir Philip Swift is here.'
On London Road to Westward
    Each member of the Bar
Fixes his gaze and there beholds
    The Judges' motor car.

And swifter, near, and swifter
    Doth the red whirlwind come
And now the car is very near
The people are afraid to cheer
But all around us we can hear
    The trampling and the hum—
Behold, from out the portals
    Two trumpeters do bring
Their trumpets. And the world around
Is made to echo with the sound
As musically they propound
    That God should save the King.

But the Circuit's face was sad
And the Circuit's speech was low
And darkly look'd they at the Hall
And darkly at the foe.
'His terrifying manner
Has won him dread renown
His ire will be upon us all
Before the sun goes down.'

Then out spake *Leo Gradwell*
That gloomy son of Fate
'To ev'ry man upon this earth
Death cometh soon or late.
And how can man die better
Than facing fearful odds
For the ashes of his fathers
And the temples of his gods.'

'Let me go in,' he pleaded,
'With all the speed I may
I, with some more to help me
Will hold the Judge in play—
In yon Crown Court, no monster,
However fierce he be
As martinet, has ever yet
Abash'd or silenced me.'

Then out spake *David Patrick*
A *Maxwell Fyfe* was he
'Lo I will stand at thy right hand
And face the foe with thee.'
And out spake *David Karmel*
An awful blood was he
'I will abide at thy left side
D'you think he'll notice me?'

Now while these three were tightening
Their bands around their necks
A wave of admiration spread
O'er others of their sex
And stuffs regaining courage
Rush'd brave to their support
And follow'd on their heels and went
Behind them into Court.

Meanwhile the mighty Rigby
    Right glorious to behold
His Clerk and marshal following
Came in like some great Eastern King
    And made my blood run cold.
Full fifty heads were lower'd
    Before that great Grandee
Who took his seat amid much dread,
All rob'd in robes of blood-like red,
And fixed his flaming eyes ahead
    Where sat the dauntless three.

And then began a battle
    The like of which I ween
Has ne'er before on Mersey's shore
    Or any shore been seen
Down went the gallant *Gradwell*
    And down went *Maxwell Fyfe*
And fighting for a felon *Karmel* yielded
                                up his life.

When at the Judge's orders
    Their bodies were remov'd
He fiercely turn'd on *Batt* and said
    'Convictions must be prov'd
And let it now be known abroad
    Throughout all Liverpool,
That, while I'm here, work must be done
With care, and not as though for fun;
And mark my words; for anyone
    Who thwarts me as a fool.'

At this the sage Professor
    Who hadn't read his brief
Felt rather like a ship must feel
    When stranded on a reef,
But with his colours flying
    Right gallantly he sank
And *Scholefield Allen* took his place
    In the fore-doom'd rank.

On seeing *Scholefield Allen*
    Sir Philip's noble brow
Frown'd such a frown that in my dreams
    I seem to see it now—

Before a word was spoken
He issued a decree
That *Allen* should be taken far
Beyond the lightship at the Bar
Where sharks and monster fishes are
And hurl'd into the sea.

Next enter'd two together
Upon that bloody field
The one was *Eric Errington*
The other *Basil Nield*
They stood there full a minute
And openly defied
The monster in the robes of red
Until at length the monster said
With emphasis I wish you dead
And then, of course, they died.

At last there rose a champion
Who stubbornly defied
Sir Philip Swift until he said
Alas, Alas I'm vanquished
I can't get through his hide.
Stein was that thick skinn'd champion
And still I seem to hear
The rapturous shout that went forth from
The Jews. And even Christendom
Could scarce forbear to cheer.

The Statue of Disraeli
Will soon be taken down
And in his stead will raise its head,
Adorn'd in wig and gown,
A new semitic figure
Of whom it shall be told
How Walter vanquish'd Philip
In the brave days of old.

Mr Junior, I move that those Stuffs whom I have mentioned in my
speech be congratulated or condoled with as the case may be.

Liverpool can claim many celebrities in the Law. One, who
originally lived his professional life in Liverpool, was Sir Noel
Goldie, Q.C., one time Conservative Member of Parliament for

Warrington, and for many years Recorder of Manchester. He, who owed all his success to Merseyside, was accustomed to saying in the train from London

'Civilization ends at Crewe and begins again at Carlisle.'

An office expected to be filled by a member of the Northern Circuit was the judgeship of the Court of Appeal in the Isle of Man. I applied for this—and let me in mitigation say that it is customary to apply for the lesser judicial offices—and soon afterwards, and again late at night in the Ayes Lobby in the House of Commons, the Home Secretary of the day, Mr Chuter Ede, approached me. He said,

'Do you really want the Isle of Man job?'

I said,

'Yes,'

and he said—

'Well, I hope you realize that it is an office of profit under the Crown, so that you will have to leave the House of Commons.'

I quickly withdrew my application.

The system of applying for appointments such as this, may seem strange. I remember sitting at lunch one day at my Inn beside two strangers. One said to the other,

'Can you tell me how one applies for a Recordership?'

His companion did not seem to know so I felt I must intervene, and I said,

'May I help you? you see I have applied for nine.'

For the future the proposal is that in Liverpool there should be a High Court and a Crown Court served by High Court and Circuit judges.

MANCHESTER

The old assize courts in Great Ducie Street were opened in 1864 and the judges who then presided were Sir Alexander Cockburn, Baronet, the Lord Chief Justice of England and Sir Gillery Pigott a Baron of the Court of Exchequer. These were excellent courts of considerable dignity and I remember, in particular, the impressive library. Adjoining the courts were the judges' rooms, including a dining-room in which members of the Bar were daily entertained to luncheon. Also adjoining the courts, was Strangeways Gaol. These courts were destroyed by

H.M. The Queen and H.R.H. Prince Philip with Lord Chief Justice Parker
at the opening of the new Courts at Manchester on 24 May 1961

H.M. The Queen, H.R.H. Prince Philip, Lord Chief Justice Parker and Lord Goddard

The opening of the new Courts at Manchester by H.M. The Queen

Lancaster House, the Lodgings, Salford: Stirling, J. and Bridge, J.

enemy action at the end of 1940 and thereafter until 24 May 1961, the judges of assize used the magistrates' courts in Minshull Street and also some rooms in the Town Hall.

The new Courts of Justice were opened by H.M. the Queen on 24 May 1961 and were the first great building of their kind to be built for a long time. The ceremony of the Royal opening was extremely impressive. It also had its lighter moments, in particular when the Queen—it being pointed out that in the criminal courts the Crown is always prosecuting so that the case is called Regina v. Smith—in the course of her speech, said that it was a tribute to the impartiality of her judges that, although in criminal cases she was always a party, she did not always win.

The judges' lodgings are at Lancaster House, Vine Street in— let it be noticed carefully—the City of Salford. It is a gravely false step to speak of the lodgings as being in Manchester. It is a large Victorian house with a bowling green upon which some of the judges insist upon disporting themselves.

When I was Recorder of Manchester, I lived at the Union Club in Mosley Street which has now been pulled down. It was an admirable institution, started in 1825 and retaining the same

Nield, J., Gorman, J., Austin Jones, J., Baker, J. at Salford Lodgings

At Salford Lodgings:
   Back row: Christopher Beresford-Jones, Nicholas Lyell (marshals)
   Front row: Payne, J., Lyell, J., Ashworth, J., Latey, J.

distinguished, if rather decaying, club house until the end. Several of us, including Mr Justice 'Bill' Gorman, lived there during the week and were inevitably referred to as 'the inmates'. We had many merry times and in the beautiful library on the first floor there could be held large dinner parties in agreeable surroundings.

During this time, one of my main interests was travelling abroad to distant places. The sort of opportunity for riposte which seldom arises, presented itself one day when the clerk to my court, my old friend, Ernest Edwards, said:

'Well, where are you going this Christmas—China?'
and I was able to reply with truth,

'No, Japan.'

If I ever attempt to write another work, I think I shall call it—with apologies to Jules Verne—'Round the World in Seventy Years'.

One of the burdens falling upon a Recorder, as second citizen, is to cope with the invitations which flow in to make speeches. I often used to tell my audience that, when I was a Member of Parliament, such invitations fell broadly into two categories. The first went something like this,

'We do hope that you will be able to fulfil this speaking engagement. Mr Winston Churchill will be in Washington, Mr Attlee is indisposed and Mr Clement Davies is addressing a mass meeting at the Albert Hall.' (Notice how astutely I hide any Party affiliation of those days.) 'You and you alone can fill the bill.'

Then there was the other category:

'We have searched high and low, the highways and the byways and you are our last hope.'

I always paid more attention to the latter form of invitation,—especially after going to speak in the place of a Minister at a bye-election in Lancashire and finding an audience of twelve: the Chairman, and, as it emerged, eleven visiting agents. The meeting was abandoned—the Secretary making the situation infinitely worse by saying to me:

'I am so sorry about this, but I can assure you that you were widely advertised.'

Another experience is worth recording, a chairman, a most kindly and courteous man, after my speech intended to say:

'We could have listened if he had gone on all night.'

But what he did say was:

'If we had listened he would have gone on all night!'

For the future the proposal is that in Manchester there should be a High Court and a Crown Court served by High Court and Circuit judges.

APPLEBY

Many members of the Northern Circuit will view with dismay the proposal—or is it now a fact—that no High Court judges or for that matter Circuit judges, will visit this county town again. In my earliest days I went regularly to the assizes at Appleby, even if the chances of a brief were slender, for the enjoyment of the charm of the town, the beauty of the countryside and the merry circuit parties which enlivened the King's Head Hotel. A close companion on such expeditions was an old Oxford friend Richard Trotter now the senior County Court judge in Liverpool.

Appleby is situated on the banks of the River Eden in the Eden Valley from which the County of Westmorland takes its name, 'the land of the people West of the moors (Pennines)'. Boroughgate, the main street of the town, sweeps down from the Castle to the Moot Hall and the Parish Church.

The assize courts, a small whitewashed building beside the river, and the gaol, were built in 1770. In recent times, the judge arrived by train, was met by the High Sheriff and escorted to his lodgings in a coach and pair. He was protected by javelin men, and footmen and two trumpeters attended, all in livery. In 1923 a posse of police took the place of the javelin men and a motor car was substituted for the coach. At that time the question was raised as to whether or no the assizes should continue to sit in Appleby; it was raised again in 1936 and it was then agreed that the judge would attend only if there was a case to be heard, and not merely to open the Commission and receive a pair of white gloves, which it is traditional to hand to him if there are no prisoners for trial.

Nicholson and Burn in 1777 record that the judge from time immemorial had been entertained at Appleby Castle, the residence of the hereditary High Sheriffs. During the Civil War, the people of Appleby remained loyal to the King and, when the Charter imposed by the Commonwealth arrived, neither

Appleby: the Low Cross, the Cloisters and St Lawrence Church

The Assize Courts, Appleby

Mr Cuthbert Acland's luncheon party at Ambleside

mayor nor bailiffs would read it. The soldiery 'Had to have recourse unto a fellow in the Market, an unclean bird, hatched at Kirby Stephen, the nest of all traitors, who proclaimed it aloud.'

By no means the least loyal of the inhabitants was the then Lady of the Manor, the Lady Anne Clifford, Countess Dowager of Pembroke, Dorset and Montgomery and 'High Sheriffess by inheritance of the County of Westmorland'. This last member of a noble family fortified Appleby Castle for the King coming North in 1649. It is recorded that Lady Anne, with her caval-cade, rode to the county boundary to receive the judge and that she sat with him when the assizes were held first at Appleby Castle and later at the Moot Hall.

In my early days Lord Hothfield owned the castle and gener-ously entertained the judge of assize there, but on his death the judge moved to the Vicarage where he was comfortably housed.

When I took the assizes in Westmorland in the summer of 1968, I was fortunate in that the High Sheriff, Mr Cuthbert

A view from Stagshaw, Ambleside

Acland, an enthusiast for the preservation of rural England, was able to show me much of the beauties of the Lake District.

Again in my early days, there were still several laymen, distinguished personalities in their county, who presided at Quarter Sessions. One of these was the then Earl of Lonsdale. He will be remembered as a great sporting peer and racehorse owner who toured the country from Lowther Castle in bright yellow coaches or motor cars. I remember him well at the Grasmere Sports, never without a cigar. His belt was and is much sought after by pugilists.

As a layman, however—and it is not surprising—Lord Lonsdale had some difficulty in summing up to a jury in a criminal trial. Unfortunately, time and again the Court of Criminal Appeal, as it then was, had to quash a conviction because the Chairman had not really got the law quite right. This being so, Lord Lonsdale wisely sought advice, and again very wisely indeed, went to see Mr Justice Lynskey, who set down on paper all the fundamental points which the Chairman should make in summing-up. At the next sitting of the Quarter Sessions at Kendal, Lord Lonsdale started to sum up splendidly: he read all the points loudly and accurately and his direction to

The author and Antony Lewis (marshal)

the jury was impeccable. Having reached the end of Mr Justice
Lynskey's invaluable note, however, the Chairman took off his
spectacles, looked long and hard at the jury and said,

'That, members of the jury, is what these lawyers say. Now
you listen to me.'

Alas—I need hardly say it—the old errors were repeated and the
Court of Criminal Appeal again constrained to point out that
this was so.

For the future the proposal is that in Appleby there should
be magistrates' courts only.

CHAPTER VII

The North-Eastern Circuit

THE North-Eastern Circuit has hitherto comprised five
Assize towns:

        Durham
        Newcastle-upon-Tyne
        Leeds
        Sheffield
        York

DURHAM

Durham, itself, dates only from the end of the tenth century
when the monks of Lindisfarne rested there with the body of
St Cuthbert. Soon afterwards, a church was built by Bishop
Ealshune, and the see was removed to Durham from Lindisfarne.
The rocky peninsula almost surrounded by the River Wear was
called Dunholm (Hill Island). The Castle was built by William
the Conqueror across the neck of the peninsula to guard the
church and monastery. In an encyclopaedia nearly 100 years
old, one reads, 'The Castle of Durham consists of a polygonal
keep, now reconstructed to form a very inconvenient set of
College rooms.' This I dare say is a justified criticism but the
building is vastly impressive. The great dining-hall, to which the
judges are often invited for dinner, built by Bishop Hatfield, has
some features finer than any of the halls in the older Universities.
The Castle was the chief palace of the Prince Bishops of the
Palatinate. However, the University was founded in 1832, the
only English collegiate and residential University beside Oxford
and Cambridge, and one of its fourteen colleges, namely
University College, now occupies the Castle, with the exception,
however, of the State rooms, which are partly reserved for the
Bishop and partly for the judges of assize. The Bishop's apart-
ments occupied by the senior judge, are magnificent and one

Procession from the Castle to the Cathedral, Durham

Procession from the Cathedral to the Castle, Durham

The Tower, Durham Castle

The Gatehouse, Durham Castle

Durham Castle

Durham Cathedral

notices how quite considerable rooms, including a bathroom off the dining room, are contained within the thickness of the Castle wall. Some say that the plumbing is still somewhat mediaeval. In the drawing-room are some notable tapestries, and it is said that some of the more timid of the judiciary would require their marshal to search behind the tapestries for intruders before retiring for the night.

The Cathedral, where the assize service is held, is, in many respects, just as Bishop William de St Calais planned it in 1092. This must surely be one of the—if not the—mightiest of all our cathedrals. The interior presents the appearance, as Dr Johnson remarked, of 'rocky solidity and of indeterminate duration,' and combines, it might be said, perfect proportions with a harmonious magnificence of detail in its massive columns, arches and stone groining.

Palace Green on top of the hill—the hill called 'Island Hill'—must, I think, be one of the most beautiful places of its kind. To the south is the Norman Cathedral, to the north the Castle and around the green many gracious houses—good examples of seventeenth- and eighteenth-century architecture—and also later buildings, some of them of Durham School, specially designed to blend in with their surroundings.

Of the Cathedral, Walter Scott wrote—and his words are to be seen on a plaque on Prebends Bridge:

> Grey Towers of Durham!
> Well yet I love thy mixed and massive piles,
> Half church to God, half castle 'gainst the Scot,
> And long to roam these venerable aisles
> With records stored of deeds long forgot.

I digress to say that I have just heard of the death of Lord Goddard, about whom I have written elsewhere in this record. He died on 29 May 1971, at his residential chambers in the Temple at the age of 94. He became a High Court judge in 1932, a Lord Justice of Appeal in 1938, a Lord of Appeal in Ordinary in 1944 and Lord Chief Justice of England in 1946, and this great office he held until his retirement in 1958. He had a reputation, especially among the criminal classes, of being a harsh and fierce judge. Those who knew him well—and I am glad to say I did—recognized that a rugged exterior hid a very warm and sympathetic personality. In court he reached a view

The Right Hon. Lord Goddard of Aldbourne, G.C.B., Lord Chief Justice
of England 1946–58

very quickly, but if counsel showed that view to be wrong, he would always discard his first opinion and have the courage and good sense to admit the initial error. Sometimes apparently rather impatient, he maintained throughout his many years of judicial life, a courtesy to all, of any station, around him which attracts, as it did in Lord Goddard's case, high regard and affection.

I think Lord Goddard might have liked to be reminded of a cartoon which appeared some years ago. It showed a dignified room in Whitehall with a conference in progress considering the methods of reforming the criminal. There is a prison Governor, a senior Probation Officer, a representative of the Lord Chancellor's office and of the Home Office, a member of After-Care organizations, and a psychiatrist. The great mahogany door is timidly opened and in looks a little old woman, grey and frail and peering from behind thick spectacles. She says—

'Please excuse me, I am sorry, but may I come in—you see I live alone, and I am frightened to go home.'

Lord Goddard throughout his immensely distinguished career strove mightily to protect those who might be victims of crime, the frightened, the hurt and the oppressed.

Returning to my subject for the future, the proposal is that in Durham there should be a Crown Court served by High Court and Circuit judges until more courts are available at Newcastle and Teeside.

NEWCASTLE-UPON-TYNE

The Romans built the first bridge across the Tyne. It was called the Bridge of Hadrian as a mark of imperial respect and was begun in A.D. 122. It was the Normans who gave Newcastle its name, for Robert Courthose, the eldest son of William the Conqueror, built the first castle here, a wooden one, in 1080. This was replaced by the present Keep and the Curtain Wall in 1177 and the Black Gate, which happily still stands, was added in 1247.

Those with interests in the Law should take a special look at the sixteenth- and seventeenth-century timbered houses in Sandhill. No. 41 was the scene of a romantic elopement in 1772 when John Scott, later Lord Eldon and Chancellor of England, put a ladder up to one of the windows one night for the descent

Lady Lawton, the author's sister and Lord Justice Lawton at 'Hadrian's Wall'

of his lady-love, Bessie Surtees, the pretty daughter of a wealthy alderman.

It is believed that justices itinerant visited Northumberland in 1166 or 1167 and thereafter at seven- or ten-yearly intervals, decreasing to three-yearly intervals from the reign of King John.

The City Commission was read in the Guild Hall on the Quayside, the County Commission was read in the Moot Hall. A change came, however, in February, 1971 when, for the first time in the history of the City and County Assize there was a combined Commission.

On this occasion the day was fine and, following the Cathedral service, there was a procession on foot from the Cathedral to the Moot Hall, a distance of about 500 yards in single file. The procession consisted of—

A Chief Superintendent of Police
The City Under Sheriff
The City Chaplain
The City Sheriff
The Clerk of the Peace
The Lord Mayor's Chaplain
The Lord Mayor
The County Under Sheriff
The High Sheriff's Chaplain
The High Sheriff of the County of Northumberland
The Clerk to the Commission
Mr Commissioner Smith
The Clerk to the Junior Judge
Mr Justice Rees
The Clerk to the Judge in Commission
The Judge in Commission, Mr Justice O'Connor
The Judge's Marshal

It is thought that this procession was appreciated by the public and indeed brought home to them that the judges were 'in town'.

A special feature of the assize at Newcastle is the holding of a function called the Dagger Dinner at which the Corporation are, in fact, the hosts but ask the judges to invite the guests. After dinner the Lord Mayor presents to the judges a gold coin: it used to be a Rose Noble, but these are now very rare and a Jacobus has taken its place. This is the dagger money with which

The Guild Hall, Newcastle-upon-Tyne

The Moot Hall, Newcastle-upon-Tyne

the judge may hire guards to protect him from highwaymen, footpads, and perhaps disappointed litigants during the perilous journey westward to the next circuit town which in early days was Carlisle. In those days, the Northern Circuit covered the country from east to west and it was later that the eastern section became the North-Eastern Circuit. In fact, when the division of the Northern Circuit into two parts was still in contemplation, it was decided that the name 'Northern' should be retained according to which side of the line Appleby fell.

It has been said that at the end of the business of the assize the Mayor or Lord Mayor would address the judges thus:

'My Lords, we have to congratulate you upon having completed your labours in this ancient town and have also to inform you that you travel hence to Carlisle, through a border country much and often infested by the Scots: we therefore present each of your lordships with a piece of money to buy therewith a dagger to defend yourselves.'

It is further said that a judge of wit once replied in this way:

'I thank the Mayor and Corporation very much for this gift. I doubt, however, whether the Scots have been so troublesome on the borders lately; I doubt too whether daggers in any numbers are to be purchased in this town for the protection of my suite and myself: and I doubt if these coins are altogether legal tender at the present time.'

Lord Justice Winn and I, with Lady Winn and my sister visited Rio de Janeiro together in the summer of 1961 and on the top of the Sugar Loaf Mountain we found a small silver dagger in a 'tourists delight' shop which we later presented to the Lady Mayoress at the Dagger Dinner, for which as tradition required we were rewarded with one half-penny each.

On the other occasion when I went to Newcastle it was agreeable to be with the Lord Chief Justice and Lady Parker. Shortly before we set out I invited the son of a High Sheriff of Norfolk, to come as my marshal to Newcastle. He accepted with apparent pleasure, but asked if he might be a day late in arriving and gave this most compelling reason: it has remained in my memory—

'You see, judge,' he said, 'for six months I have been committed, on the first day of the assize—to shooting pink footed geese on the Solway Firth with the Bishop of Sodor and Man.'

Lord Justice Winn

The Mansion House, Jesmond Dene, Newcastle-upon-Tyne

As a marshal Edward Evans-Lombe was a great success, although his six foot seven attending five foot eight made the latter look less dignified than he should.

The judges' lodgings here are at Jesmond Dene in a very fine house which is also the Mansion House, presented to the City by a one-time Lord Mayor.

One feels in these parts that there is a very deep-seated local pride in the City and the County. The Under Sheriff, during my last visit, told me of the applicant for a post with the Corporation, who was warned of this intense pride in the City. Sure enough the first question from the Selection Committee was:

'Do you know this City?'

The candidate primed, as I have indicated, said,

'Indeed I do Sir, I was at school here for quite a time.'

'Do you know the local people at all?'

'I think I can say very well, you see, Sir, I married a local girl.'

'And do you know Bishop Auckland?'

'Yes,' said the wretched victim, 'in fact, Sir, he married us.'

For the future the proposal is that in Newcastle there should be a High Court and a Crown Court served by High Court and Circuit judges.

LEEDS

A reference to Leeds was made in the eighth century by the Venerable Bede in his Ecclesiastical History stating that Edwin, King of Northumbria, built a Royal Palace at 'a place which is called Loidis.' In 1207 a Charter was granted to the burgesses of Leeds and there was laid out a wide street which, as Briggate, still remains one of the city's main arteries.

John Leland, Henry VIII's librarian, had this to say about the town in the sixteenth century:

'Ledis, two miles lower than Christal Abbey on Aire Ryver, is a praty market, having one Paroche Churche, reasonably welle buildid, and as large as Bradeford, but not so quik as it. The town stondith most by clothing.'

Perhaps he can be blamed for the rivalry between Leeds and Bradford which has flourished ever since, to the great satisfaction of the inhabitants of both places.

The assizes are held in the Town Hall which was designed in 1858 and has a commanding clock tower. Within is the Victoria Hall where concerts are held but not I need hardly say, at the time of the assizes.

The judges' lodgings are at Carr Manor, a large house in a beautiful garden on the outskirts of the town. The house was owned, and probably built, by the first Lord Moynihan, the Royal Physician.

In the large cities there is always a great deal of civil business to be dealt with and by far the greatest number of cases are claims for personal injuries suffered in road or industrial accidents. Sometimes these claims are much inflated and may be highly spurious.

It is said that there was one such case where the plaintiff's claim included the allegation that his sight was badly affected and, indeed, almost lost by reason of the accident. The defendants required a medical report and arranged for the plaintiff to be examined by a distinguished eye specialist. Arrived in his surgery, the plaintiff was asked, as usual, if he could read the top line of bold letters on the board. To this he replied he could not see the board, let alone the letters. At the end of the examination the plaintiff groped his way to the door, closed it

The Town Hall, Leeds

Carr Manor, Leeds

behind him and then walked smartly down the stairs, out into the street and into the nearby News Cinema. It happened that the eye specialist had a cancellation of one of his appointments and, wishing to see how the Test Match was progressing, he dropped into the News Cinema too and sat in the seat next but one to the plaintiff. Was the plaintiff disconcerted? Not at all. He leaned over and said,

'Excuse me madam, this is, is it not, the 'bus for Sheepscar Beck?'

For the future the proposal is that in Leeds there should be a High Court and a Crown Court served by High Court and Circuit judges.

SHEFFIELD

The country in which Sheffield is situated was described by Sir Osbert Sitwell in this way:

On one side is Hallamshire from which during the passing of centuries has been born a great industrial district—on the other, the hills and dales of Derbyshire with their druidical remains, with their quarries of blue john and of grey marble, with their gushing mineral waters and petrifying streams, with their thousand lingering tradition of Sherwood Forest—which not so long ago extended into our countryside as far as Chatsworth—and of the Peak where the playing of the bagpipes lingered on until the sixteenth century.

In this wide country, the most typical feature is the splendour of its houses, Hardwick, Welbeck, Bolsover Castle and Chatsworth, Wentworth Woodhouse and Haddon.

Sheffield was the capital of Hallamshire from the time of the Norman Conquest and the Manor passed to the Barons of Huntingdon, one of whom had a castle at Sheffield.

The reference to Hallamshire is to be noted. Sheffield was made an assize town as recently as 1955. In June of that year, the assizes there were opened by Lord Goddard, then Lord Chief Justice. For the next seven years the High Sheriff of Yorkshire was expected to attend the three Yorkshire Assize towns, York, Leeds and Sheffield. In 1962, however, following the recommendations of the Committee under the chairmanship of Mr Justice Streatfeild, to which reference is made elsewhere, Sheffield became a separate Assize County with its own High Sheriff, known as the High Sheriff of Hallamshire.

Naturally one's mind turns to the cutlers when looking at Sheffield's history. It is certain that the town had become famous for its cutlers by the fourteenth century as is shown by an allusion to it in Chaucer. In Queen Elizabeth I's reign an important trade in knives was carried on and the Cutlers Company was incorporated in 1624. The Cutler's Hall was built in 1832 and enlarged in 1857.

It seemed to be frequently the case that the judges were offered a box at the theatre in Sheffield and so to enjoy an evening's relaxation. It was often the custom too to invite some of the leading actors back to supper at the lodgings. The story is told that one most talented actress who professed to being practically a teetotaller and was in truth something of a tippler, was sometimes among the guests. Invited to take a glass of whisky at the lodgings she would at first decline saying:

'I hardly ever take anything, don't you know.'

Pressed to make this an exceptional occasion she would say:

'Well, if you really insist, I'll have just a teeny weeny double.'

The Town Hall, Sheffield

Whirlow Court, near Sheffield

The assizes hitherto have sat in the Town Hall and the judges are lodged in a large and comfortable house at Whirlow some way from the town out towards the Derbyshire Moors.

For the future the proposal is that in Sheffield there should be a High Court and a Crown Court served by High Court and Circuit judges.

YORK

In York, the centre of the Archbishop's See, one turns at once to view that wonderful example of English ecclesiastical architecture, the Minster. It is said to occupy the site of a wooden church of the seventh century. According to Bede, King Edwin thereafter began to construct 'a large and more noble basilica of stone.' Passing through many troubles, the building as it is now seen, dates in the main from the years 1154 to 1256. As in the case of so many of our treasures of architecture, the Minster is in great need of funds for its maintenance and repair. When I was last there, there were cavernous holes in the floor where cement was being injected into the foundations of the great pillars by men in steel helmets looking very much like coal miners. Let us hope to be able to make safe and sure this great church.

In York, too, one turns soon to the Castle, but it seems doubtful if any part of the fortress built by William the Conqueror remains. The later building became a prison. Within the present Castle walls are the assize courts built in 1777, a fine example of eighteenth-century architecture by the well known York architect, Carr. Both courts have fine domes decorated with plaster work. In all probability, the very earliest of the justices in Eyre sat in York.

The City of York has its own Sheriff so that there are two Commissions; one for the County and one for the City. The City Commission is read in the ancient Guildhall, a mediaeval building next to the Mansion House. In 1942 York was one of the victims of what were called the Baedeker air raids in which the enemy sought to destroy some of the places of special beauty and historical interest in the land, and the Guildhall suffered greatly. It was, however, restored after the War, the fine oak pillars being made from oak trees given by various landowners in the county.

Civic pride is as understandable as it is noticeable, in the

The Minster and Guildhall, York

City. The City plate which the judges are often invited to view, is quite outstanding. The Lord Mayor is entitled to be addressed as 'The Right Honourable' and wears a black and gold robe similar to that of the Lord Mayor of London. Equally, the City is hospitable and generous. It used to be the custom for the judges to be invited on the first day of the assize to breakfast at the Mansion House. I rather think I was, in a measure, instrumental in having this function changed to luncheon, since I doubt if most people are at their best at breakfast time. It is also the custom of the Lady Mayoress of the day to present each of the judges with a silver vinaigrette. With all respect to the City, I expect this began when the vinaigrette was filled with sweet smelling herbs to fend off the odour of the crowd, or, indeed, the danger of the Plague, just as for these purposes, the posies of herbs are presented to the judges at the Old Bailey and in some other places.

On the first Sunday of each assize there is an assize service in the Minster, after which the High Sheriff usually gives a luncheon party.

The Castle, York

The judges' lodgings are a delightful eighteenth-century house which was built by a Dr Wintringham, a forbear of Sir Wintringham Stable who was a Queen's Bench judge for some twenty-five years. In the dining-room a sliding door in the panelling reveals the presence of a china 'article' which no doubt—before the gentlemen joined the ladies after dinner— saved a journey to other parts of the house.

My only critical note (not a real one) is that the quiet of the lodgings is disturbed at all hours by the strange cries of the peacocks in the nearby Park.

Two happenings stand out in my memory of visits to York. Mr Justice Austin Jones, who was a pupil of F. E. Smith in Liverpool—and it follows of great seniority—was with me on the assize during which H.R.H. the Duke of Kent was married to Miss Worsley at the Minster. My brother judge always said that my entry relating to this event in the Lodgings Book made it look as if we attended the ceremony, whereas in fact we were not invited. Let me say that I did not intend to dissemble in this way and hasten to add that, as the Queen was in the County, we

The Lodgings, York

could not sit in our courts and that we spent much time gazing from behind our curtains at the various notabilities who had been invited.

The other happening gave me special pleasure. I was the first judge of assize to be invited officially by the newly established University of York to dine, as it were, at the High Table. The appropriate building was not completed—indeed it may not have been begun—and so 'the High Table' was the Yorkshire Club where the Vice Chancellor presided. It was Lord James of Rusholme who was kind enough to arrange this and I was glad to recall our many earlier meetings when he was High Master of the Manchester Grammar School and I was in charge of the Crown Court in that city.

For the future the proposal is that in York there should be a High Court and a Crown Court served by High Court and Circuit judges until more courts are available at Leeds.

CHAPTER VIII

The Oxford Circuit

T HE Oxford Circuit, which, to the regret of its members, ceases to exist as such under the Beeching plan, embraced eight Assize towns—

Reading
Gloucester
Hereford
Newport (Monmouthshire)
Oxford
Shrewsbury
Stafford
Worcester

READING

In the Anglo-Saxon Chronicle there is an account of the occupation of Reading by the invading Danes in 871. Some 250 years later, Henry I founded Reading Abbey, which was one of the largest Benedictine monasteries in England. It is clear that, at the Abbey, the Abbot had great power. It was he, for example, who chose the Warden of Reading's Merchant Guild from three candidates presented to him by the burgesses. For long the burgesses struggled to be free from the Abbot's domination. This freedom came with the dissolution of the Monastery and, indeed, the last Abbot was hanged outside his own gateway in 1539. Henry VIII granted a Charter to the town and powers were given to the borough. Of special interest here, one notes that one of the powers was to hold a weekly Court of Record to deal with small offences and the borough was permitted to maintain a prison: thus opening the way for the famous ballad.

The county of Berkshire is indeed a beautiful part of England and the Thames Valley a delight to visit. At Wallingford one

An old print of Reading

sees Castle Priory House, once the home of the great English Law historian, Sir William Blackstone.

Being but forty minutes by train from Paddington, the members of the Bar travel to and fro each day and do not have any circuit life in Reading in the ordinary course of things. After a particularly heavy criminal case, which lasted some eight weeks and involved some seven Queen's Counsel, the Bar invited me to dinner and entertained me lavishly. The occasion stays in my memory specially because the Leader of the Oxford Circuit, now Judge Alan King-Hamilton, was appointed a judge of the Central Criminal Court during the case and had to leave it rather abruptly to take up his important appointment.

During the dinner party a member of the Circuit surprised us all by asking if we knew that the great Mr Gulbenkian—several times a millionaire—had once had a cheque returned. It was drawn upon some foreign bank for a modest $4\frac{1}{2}$ millions and after a day or so the Bank returned it marked 'Returned for lack of funds—not you—us'.

For the future the proposal is that in Reading there should be a Crown Court served by High Court and Circuit judges.

GLOUCESTER

Like so many assize towns, Gloucester can trace its history back to the very earliest times. At about the time when the justices in eyre began to go on circuit, Henry II granted a Charter, dated 1155, bestowing on Gloucester liberties and privileges similar to those of Westminster and Parliaments were frequently summoned to Gloucester.

It is said that the building known as the Booth Hall in Westgate Street was used from time immemorial by the County and the City jointly for their assizes, Quarter Sessions and other courts and for elections. A County meeting convened in January 1803 resolved that a new Shire Hall be built, the Booth Hall being dilapidated and insecure. On 28 July the project was adjourned in view of 'the unexpected political events that intervened' (this was the threat of invasion by Napoleon). The present Shire Hall was built between 1813 and 1820. Within it the great vestibule leads to the staircase rising to the great Hall and to the pair of courts which were highly praised by the first judge to preside there.

Up a narrow passage, once called Maverdine Lane, is a portion of the front of an old house. It is a fine specimen of domestic architecture and on the chimney-piece in one of the panelled rooms appears the text 'I and my House will serve the Lord' and it is dated 1633. The house is usually called the 'Old Judge's House'. I can imagine if someone were asked who lives there now there might be produced as an answer an excellent example of a *non sequitur* 'the old judge, I suppose'. The house, however, is more famous as the house from which Colonel Massie issued his orders in 1643 when Gloucester was besieged by Charles I. During the nineteenth century the judges' lodgings were moved first to Ribston Hall, and later to a pair of Regency houses where they still are and in which I have enjoyed staying.

No doubt improvements in the accommodation for the judge were prompted by the acid observations of Mr Justice Maule in April 1847 when he intimated that, while he was anxious to expedite the business of the assizes, the court would not open for business before half-past nine each morning (the courts then

The Shire Hall, Gloucester

sat much earlier than they do now) that extra half hour being requisite for him to travel from Cheltenham where he was obliged to go each evening,

> 'finding it impossible to sleep in the unventilated, undrained, foetid dog-hole which the liberality of the magistrates of Gloucester had provided as lodgings for Her Majesty's Justices of Assize. People of robust health might struggle through these inconveniences without risk to their lives, but he was obliged to seek in an inn at Cheltenham that accommodation which was denied him at Gloucester.'

The City of Gloucester is, by Charter, a county in itself. Thus, there is a Sheriff who is appointed by the City Council, but is an Officer of the Crown. He attends the assizes, as of course does the High Sheriff of the county.

At Gloucester the Dean is good enough in the usual course of things, to arrange an assize service in the Cathedral on the first Sunday after the assize opens. This, as in some other cathedrals, is a State occasion when the judges put on their State robes—the scarlet robe, the ermine hood and over it the ermine mantle—knee breeches, buckled shoes and full bottom wig. Met at the west door by the clergy and the choir, the

The Lodgings, Gloucester

Gloucester Cathedral

procession moves forward, the High Sheriff and his chaplain preceding the judges who come last save for the judges' marshal. I note in passing that the present Lord Chancellor, Lord Hailsham of St Marylebone, as Mr Quintin Hogg was a judge's marshal in Gloucester in the early 1930s.

How does one feel when all this pomp and panoply surrounds one? For myself, I feel first, humble, and surprised that I should be the centre of all this ceremonial and one upon whom all eyes are fixed. Next I feel pride that, after many years, I have reached a position of some eminence so as to be a central figure here. How can these two different feelings be reconciled? I am certain the solution is to be found when it is realized that the dignity attaches not to the man but to the office. All this respect is for the Court and not the holder of the judicial office.

About thirteen years ago, the Lord Chief Justice of England, the late Lord Goddard, retired from office after many years of judicial greatness. I happened to meet him in the Temple one day and raised my hat.

'Now then,' he said, assuming that apparent gruffness which

was wholly alien to his nature, 'don't you take your hat off to
me, I'm only an old Has Been.'
I said:
'Sir, I know that usually one removes one's hat in deference
to the office and not to the man: in the present case I take it off
to the man and, what is more, I shall continue to do so.'
Thus did I delight to defy the injunction of a great man and a
close friend.

For the future the proposal is that in Gloucester there should
be a Crown Court served by High Court and Circuit judges.

HEREFORD

Herefordshire claims to be one of the counties which has not
been disfigured by the march of progress and to have changed
little in appearance for many centuries. Hereford itself, on the
banks of the River Wye, was of much strategic value as being at
the approaches to the land of the hostile mountain tribes of
Wales. This was appreciated in early days by Offa, King of the
Mercians, who built Offa's Dyke along the border of Wales. In
the thirteenth century a castle was built at Hereford and regarded
by Leland as 'one of the fayrest, largest and strongest royal
Castles in England'.

There is a very early history of courts established in Herefordshire. King Athelstan held a great meeting with the Welsh
princes at Hereford and is said to have fixed the River Wye as
the boundary between England and Wales. Laws, which were
issued at this time, laid down that neither English nor Welsh
were to cross the river without an official guide in order to
make sure that they returned safely without committing any
offence, but, if either an Englishman or a Welshman was killed
on the wrong side of the river, only half 'the death price' need
be paid. Welsh people kept their own laws and customs until
after the Norman Conquest, but courts were held for them at
Wormelow and the citizens had to provide the Sheriff with a
bodyguard when he went to hold them. This, I suppose, was an
early form of 'Dagger money' which is still given to the judges
in Newcastle-upon-Tyne.

The judge has an attractive house as his lodgings near to the
cathedral and let for this purpose by a Hereford solicitor.

At one time it was the custom of the Corporation of Ludlow

The Cathedral, Hereford

to offer hospitality to the judges. It took the form of cakes presented on a silver salver, and wine in a loving cup, offered by the representatives of the town to the judges, on the train carrying them from Shrewsbury to Hereford when it stopped at Ludlow. In 1858 this agreeable custom ceased. Mr Justice Hill wrote to the Mayor saying:

'Owing to the delay occasioned, Her Majesty's judges would not stop at Ludlow to receive the wonted hospitality.'

The Mayor and Corporation were offended and did not offer to renew the ceremony.

For the future the proposal is that in Hereford there should be a Crown Court served by Circuit judges.

NEWPORT (MONMOUTHSHIRE)

Mr W. John Collett writes that Newport was probably originally called Castell Newydd after the Norman Castle which was erected on the bank of the Usk to guard the lowest fordable place.

A Norman lordship was set up with its centre at Newport

The City Hall and Law Courts, Newport

Castle and to it were added a number of sub-manors in South Monmouthshire. The Castle was built about 1126—first of wood, later of stone. In 1402 Owen Glendower reduced the Castle, burnt the town and destroyed the bridge.

In 1536 came the Act of Union between England and Wales and the various lordships were formed into the county of Monmouthshire.

An early case at the Monmouth assizes was that of Zephaniah Williams, William Jones and John Frost (who had been Mayor of Newport in 1836). These three men led bands of workers aiming to seize Newport and start a rising in order to form a new Government to try to improve economic conditions and the lot of the working man. A riot developed, but the rioters were driven off. The leaders stood their trial for treason and were transported to Tasmania. Frost was later pardoned and lived to be 93. It was down Stow Hill that these Chartists marched—they were drunken and riotous and troops opened fire upon them. Bullet marks are still to be seen at the entrance of an hotel at the bottom of the hill.

The assize service was held at St Woolos Cathedral on Stow Hill, a church which retains fine Norman features. It is of interest to realize that my fellow-Bencher of the Inner Temple, Sir Frank Soskice, took his title from Stow Hill when he was made a peer, having before that represented Newport in the House of Commons for a number of years, during which he became Solicitor-General and Attorney-General.

The assize courts are in the Civic Centre, a very fine new building.

The judges' lodgings are in the Mansion House so that I fear we put the Mayor to some inconvenience.

When I was last in Newport the High Sheriff was Colonel Harry Llewellyn and he took me to the top of a high mountain to show me the grave of his famous horse, Foxhunter.

It was also at Newport that I succeeded, and perhaps this is unique, in marrying off my marshal to the daughter of an ex-High Sheriff. The marshal was David Johnson and he married Julia, the daughter of Colonel and Mrs Somerset Hopkinson.

For the future the proposal is that in Newport there should be a Crown Court served by Circuit judges only.

OXFORD

An eighteenth-century writer, calling himself 'a gentleman of Oxford', wrote a guide to Oxford and the University and of the town he wrote—

> The town is situated on a broad eminence, which arises so gradually as to be hardly perceptible, in the midst of a most beautiful extent of meadows to the south east and west, and of cornfields to the north. The vales on the east are watered by the River Cherwell, and those on the west and south by the main stream, and several branches of the Isis (Thames).
>
> The landscape is bounded on every side, the north excepted, by a range of hills covered with woods. From some of the surrounding hills, the traveller is surprised with an unparalleled prospect of magnificence and plenty of numerous spires, domes and turrets, with the combined charm of verdure, water and trees.

The first appearance of Oxford in recorded history is the reference in the *Anglo-Saxon Chronicle* of A.D. 912 to the effect that on the death of Ethelred, Ealdoman of the Mercians, 'King Edward took possession of London and of Oxford and of all the lands which owed obedience thereto.' Thus, the town can claim a much greater antiquity than the University, the first records of which appeared in the twelfth and thirteenth centuries.

As you make your way from the railway station towards Carfax, you pass the remains of a place probably even more ancient than either the town or the University: Oxford Castle. Of the original castle nothing remains, but the Mound is probably Norman. It is clear from a pamphlet on the *Ancient Remains of Oxford Castle* by R. H. Gretton, published in 1924 that, at all times, the castle, which in the earliest days was really a small walled town, embraced the Sessions House where the courts were held, and a prison and a gallows. The use of the castle as a prison can be traced as far back as the reign of Henry III and from the 1500s, at any rate, this had become its main purpose.

The Sessions House ceased to be used for the holding of the assizes after the grim events of what came to be known as the Black Assize. At the assize in 1577, gaol fever broke out with such virulence that most of the people concerned in the assize died. They included two judges, the Clerk of Assize, the Coroner, the High Sheriff, the Under Sheriff, three of the Grand Jury, all but two of another jury and sixteen persons who were probably Justices of the Peace. Over a hundred undergraduates also died.

The present assize courts, near to the Mount and adjoining the prison, were built in 1841 and were termed by Sir Charles Oman 'quite the most abominable pseudo-gothic Assize Court in England.'

Abominable or no, this was the first assize court I ever visited. A close friend and fellow-undergraduate was one, Maurice Lush, who unhappily died a few months ago. He took me to listen to the proceedings when his father, Mr Justice Montague Lush, was presiding. My next visit was rather more than forty years on when I, myself, was presiding. This let me admit it, thrilled me.

On this latter visit, I arrived with my marshal, Peter Newell, at the judges' lodgings in my quite modest motor car to find a young police officer on duty. He asked me my business and, when told, seemed rather abashed saying:

'I am sorry, my Lord, I had expected you to be driven here in a large Rolls-Royce.'

I was presented with the traditional white gloves edged with

The Courts, the Castle, Oxford

The Lodgings, St Giles, Oxford

gold lace cuffs, one pair from the City and the other from the University, and attended the assize service at St Mary's, the University Church, on the first day of the sittings with the Vice-Chancellor supported by his retinue.

In those days the judge was lodged in a most beautiful and distinguished house in St Giles, at one time the town house of the Dukes of Marlborough and now owned by St John's College, and it was agreeable to entertain there to dinner some of the heads of Houses. However, during my time there, St John's wanted the house back and so the Under Sheriff and county officials were seeking another lodging. They had chosen Shotover Park, a large and handsome house some six miles to the north of the city and the middle of an estate of some 1,800 acres. My sister and I were asked by the Under Sheriff, Mr Gerald Burkitt, to visit the house so as to make any suggestions as to how that part of the house to be used as judges' lodgings should be arranged. On arrival, I was indeed pleased to find that I knew the owner, Major Miller, quite well and we had met, in fact, when he was stationed at Western Command.

Shotover was started to be built in 1710 by one General James Tyrell with the advice of Hawksmoor and Vanbrugh.

Shotover Park, near Oxford

I feel that the judges are fortunate to be housed in so attractive a place.

For the future the proposal is that in Oxford there should be a Crown Court served by High Court and Circuit judges.

SHREWSBURY

Shrewsbury is an attractive town and Shropshire a beautiful county. For two hundred years after the coming of the Normans, Shrewsbury was a frontier fortress and a centre of feudal government and administration in the no-man's land of the Welsh Marches.

It is probably correct to say that assizes have been held in Shrewsbury since the time of Henry II. The great Shropshire historian, R. W. Eyton, in his earliest reference to Salop Assizes in 1221, recalls that Edward I removed the whole of his administration, including the courts, from Westminster to Shrewsbury in 1282.

The Corporation of Shrewsbury's records contain this entry of 10 April 1727:

> Whereas the several gilds and innkeepers have withdrawn their contributions towards entertaining the judges—AGREED that for the future the Corporation expend no more money on that account. The judges of Assize were refused the usual compliments by the Mayor. On this account the next Assizes were held at Bridgnorth. This was a point long contested between the judges and the Corporation and the dispute was not settled as late as 1738 when the assizes were held at Bridgnorth, it is believed, for the last time.

In 1783 at the summer assizes the judge complained of the inadequacy of the court and threatened to impose a fine of £2,000. The magistrates were much aggrieved, but had to comply.

The assizes up to 1967 were held in the various Shire Halls. The County archivist, Miss Mary Hill, has written a most interesting history of Shropshire's many Shire Halls. She writes of the first guild, or Booth Hall, which was seized by Edward II on the grounds that the burgesses had built it illegally. The burgesses pointed out that their Charter empowered them 'to improve the town.' A second Shire Hall was built in 1452, a third in 1783 and a fourth in 1833.

The Castle, Shrewsbury

The fourth Shire Hall was burnt down in 1880—there being considerable adverse comment as to the manner in which the fire brigade sought to deal with the outbreak. This reference to a fire brigade recalls an example of the importance of punctuation. The statement appeared in a well-known provincial weekly newspaper recording an outbreak of fire, that—

> The blaze was put out before any very serious damage could be done by the local fire brigade.

Finally the new Shire Hall was built to house the courts and nearly all the services of the Salop County Council near to the column erected in 1816 in honour of Lord Hill, Wellington's right-hand man in the Peninsular War, and this Hall was opened by the Queen in 1967.

The judge's lodging at No. 6 Belmont is a distinguished house. It was built in 1701 by Jonathan Scott who lived at Betton. His object in building No. 6 Belmont was to have a town house for occasional residence and a property qualification within the borough which would give him a vote for Shrewsbury as well as for Shropshire. This custom of having a town house within the walls of a provincial city is quite common. Macaulay wrote—

The Shire Hall, Shrewsbury

6 Belmont, Shrewsbury: John Dalton (marshal)

In the language of the gentry many miles round the Wrekin, to go to Shrewsbury was to go to town. The provincial wits and beauties imitated, as well as they could, the fashions of St James's Park in the walks along the side of the Severn.

One well-known trial at Shrewsbury should be mentioned. At the spring assizes in 1757, thirty seven colliers were tried for rioting in a time of great scarcity. Four died in gaol and ten were condemned to death. The judge, however, sent a report by express to the Attorney-General, naming four only to be executed. The report lay untouched on Mr Pitt's desk until after the date fixed for the execution. However, the Under Sheriff, Mr Egerton Leeke of Wellington, convinced that the judge had not intended that ten of the convicted men should be hanged, on his own responsibility delayed the execution until he had sent a letter, also by express, to London. Lord Chief Justice Willis was afraid to tell the King, but was greatly relieved to find that the execution had been delayed. Mr Leeke was highly commended and only four of the ten men were hanged.

It remains to record that, if the judge visits Shrewsbury during Term time, he may still have to contend, as he does in some other places, with a Latin letter from the boys of the famous school, requesting a holiday.

For the future the proposal is that in Shrewsbury there should be a Crown Court served by High Court and Circuit judges.

STAFFORD

The county handbook proudly names seven sons of Staffordshire, who have left a particular mark on the county; of these I mention two as of special interest to the Law and to Letters.

In 1709 Samuel Johnson was born at Lichfield, the son of a book-seller. He was unsuccessful as a young man, left Oxford after four terms and was not happy as a school-master. For many years he was an underpaid writer and he received recognition only in 1755 when his famous dictionary was published. Samuel Johnson's Scottish biographer, James Boswell was a member of the Northern Circuit and held office as Junior.

David Garrick was born in Hereford where his father, in the army, happened to be stationed, but his was a Lichfield family. He was a pupil of Samuel Johnson at Edial School. They became friends and Garrick, having achieved, quite soon, fame in the world of the theatre, produced a tragedy written by Johnson called 'Irene'. Sad to say it ran for only nine nights. Garrick intended to go to the Bar but the stage claimed him.

Looking at some of the legal history of Stafford, I have been much interested to read a short monograph written by Mr S. A. H. Burn, formerly of the Oxford Circuit, upon the remarkable continuity of the practice of a firm of solicitors, Messrs Hand Morgan and Owen, a firm which has produced many Under Sheriffs for the county of Staffordshire. The first solicitor or attorney to be referred to was a Mr John Hickin (1730–1762). He travelled much to visit clients, but was always at home on market days ready to advise the rustics in any dilemma put to him. I am not sure if the Law Society would approve in these days, but Mr Hickin seems to have invited business thus:

> You know our office, come with me and look
> This very point is in the Statute book
> Confirmed by fifty judges dead and gone
> Each wiser in his time than Solomon.

The earliest Under Sheriff from this firm, for certain, appeared in 1781 and the firm provides the Under Sheriff today.

High Sheriffs, at one time, were expected to provide javelin men to attend and, if need be, to protect the judge of assize, but they could scarcely be said to be on active service. There is an instance, however, when they were. In September 1830, a party of men occupied an isolated farmhouse at Blymill saying that they had permission to take possession of it on behalf of a man named Cowley, to whose ancestors the whole Parish of Blymill had been given under the will of King Charles II for services rendered. Here the men remained for eight days to the alarm of the widow occupant and the neighbourhood. Then the sheriff's officer came with a force of twelve javelin men 'their halberds glittering in the sun' and the same number of special constables. The intruders were ejected and many arrested, five of whom were convicted on a charge of riot at the October Sessions.

At Stafford, the assize court is in the Shire Hall and so are the judge's lodgings.

I recall on one occasion sitting there with my brother, Mr Justice Cantley. He tells me that arriving at the appropriate door of the lodgings, he found a young police officer on duty.

The Shire Hall, Stafford

Uncertain if he had come to the right place, the judge leaned out of his car and asked the officer:

'Are these the judges' lodgings?'

to which the reply came

'Yes, but they haven't come yet.'

'You're wrong, Officer, one of them has.'

In judges' lodgings there is usually a Visitors' Book in which the judges are expected to write their comments on the comfort, or otherwise, of their accommodation. It has been my custom however, if opportunity offers, to record some event in history which will be of interest to those who come after.

In 1965 I recorded these few lines in the lodgings' Book—

At the Assize Service a prayer was said for the life of Winston Spencer Churchill, a life which ended on the 24th January, 1965. All here are greatly saddened by the passing of this legendary figure.

For the future the proposal is that in Stafford there should be a High Court and a Crown Court served by High Court and Circuit judges until more courts are available at Birmingham, Coventry and Stoke-on-Trent.

WORCESTER

It is said that Worcester is one of the oldest assize towns in the country, the judges having been coming to the City and County Assizes since 1170. The earliest documents of assize in the Record Office are those of Worcester dating back to 1221. It is yet another beautiful cathedral city which judges of the High Court have been privileged to visit and it is sad that under the new arrangements, they will no longer do so.

Among the records there appears the account of the trial in 1606 of the Jesuit, Father Edward Oldcorne, who was arraigned on charges in connection with the Gunpowder Plot. He was found guilty of treason and hanged on Red Hill.

Mr J. B. Matthews, who was a solicitor in Worcester, wrote for the *Berrows Worcester Journal* a short series of articles about some recorded trials and was prompted to do so as a member of the Seldon Society. He told of a case in which a jury found that a woman called Emma had been drowned, whereas in fact she had been murdered by her husband Roger. The jurors were proceeded against for giving a false verdict, for which they were liable to be fined. It is strange to us in these days to think that this could happen: many verdicts may be perverse, but there is little to be done about it.

If one looks back three hundred and fifty years, the Oxford Circuit and its assize towns were the same then as they are today, save that Newport is now the assize town for Monmouthshire instead of Monmouth.

In Worcestershire the High Sheriff in his State coach, with the Mayor of Worcester and other dignitaries, would drive to the top of Red Hill to meet the judge and his retinue and escort them to the cathedral. A man was stationed on the cathedral tower to give notice of the approach of the party when the bells were immediately rung.

Although an Order in Council in February 1574 relieved the sheriff from the charge of the judge's diet, yet sheriffs and mayors and others sent in presents of provisions of startling proportions. In 1601 the presents included $6\frac{1}{2}$ bucks, 4 lambs, 2 muttons, a pheasant, partridges, ducks, chickens etc.

On the morning of the day upon which the assizes opened, the High Sheriff gave a breakfast and afterwards, with his guests and accompanied by trumpeters, mounted javelin men and a troup of horsemen, set out to meet the judge.

In court the Grand Jury did their work after being charged by the judge and they inserted their findings in a long fishing-rod-like kind of pole with pincers at the end which is referred to elsewhere and, with this in hand, in the High Gallery, the foreman projected the findings down towards the Clerk of Assize—this required considerable skill, and continued until 1933 when Grand Juries were abolished.

In the north it was the custom among members of the Grand Jury to fine each other in the interest of charity. It was said, for example, that Mr Jones' tie was too bright and he was fined £5, or Mr Smith's waistcoat unsuitable—fined £10. My father, was fined on one occasion because no-one could find any fault with him!

Worcester's splendid cathedral brings to mind in how many churches the acoustics are very poor—this I recall, is not so in Worcester Cathedral—but when advising young men who are going to the Bar, one's first words are—

'For goodness sake speak up'.

The Cathedral, Worcester

The Shirehall, Worcester

The older the judge, the more counsel mumble and I try to fix it
in their minds by saying:

'Remember the verger who was conducting the visiting
prelate to the pulpit and in a hissing whisper, which was about
the only thing that could be heard in the far side of the nave,
said: "Pray speak up My Lord, the agnostics here are something terrible." '

The judge's lodgings in Worcester are at the back of the Shire
Hall and contain magnificent, large entertaining rooms and an
attractive central staircase from the hall to the first floor.

For the future the proposal is that in Worcester there should
be a Crown Court served by Circuit judges only.

CHAPTER IX

The Wales and Chester Circuit

T HIS circuit included fourteen assize towns:

> Beaumaris
> Brecon
> Caernarvon
> Lampeter
> Carmarthen
> Chester
> Ruthin
> Mold
> Cardiff
> Swansea
> Dolgellau
> Welshpool
> Haverfordwest
> Presteigne

BEAUMARIS

The island of Anglesey has been known to me for many years. Approached as it is by the famous Telford bridge built in 1826 and the tubular railway bridge built in 1850, which was much damaged by fire in 1970, the island is a county with county offices at Llangefni. The assize court is at Beaumaris. Beaumaris borders the westerly shore of the Menai Straits and is a charming little town. Beaumaris used to boast that theirs was the oldest assize court in use in the British Isles and the small white-washed building near the castle is dated 1641. It must also, I think, have the smallest retiring room for the judge in the British Isles, being a sort of round well at the bottom of steep steps and, I would say, roughly seven feet across.

The Assize Court, Beaumaris

Nesta Evans in *Religion and politics in mid-eighteenth century Anglesey* has described the work undertaken by Chief Justices and Second Justices of the Great Sessions in the island of Anglesey. She writes:

> The Quarter Sessions were timed to fall on the same date as the Great Sessions; the prospective candidates for Parliament did some preliminary canvassing for votes, but chiefly it was a time of dinners and balls. Regular official dinners were given, the judge, all the Council and the officers of the Court dined with the Grand Jury one evening and on the next the Grand Jury dined with the judge and both entertained and were entertained by the Sheriff.

The authoress further writes of sentences:

> This reluctance on the part of the prosecutors, Grand Jury, and Petty Jury, to bring criminals to justice were based to a great extent on the same cause, the inordinate severity of the sentences in the 18th century, when burning, transportations and even death were ordained for criminals convicted of different forms of theft.

The behaviour of the judges was far from favourably commented upon. In the Bulkeley Diary an entry on the 25 April 1734 reads:

Bryn Mel, near Beaumaris, Anglesey

I had like to have forgot that there was very little business to be done in all the Sessions Week, and what there was, half of it was not done, but put off to ye next Sessions occasioned by Martyn the judge being almost continually drunk and afterwards lying in bed till 10 or 11 o'clock every day.

and on the 10 April 1741:

Though this is the last day of the Sessions the Court sat to try cases till 3 in the evening: a thing never known before in the memory of man, Martyn the judge being every day drunk, deferred all business to the last, when they were huddled over in a very unbecoming manner.

Justices of the peace were introduced into the whole of Wales in 1542. There is a reference in 1549 to the holding of Quarter Sessions in the town of Beaumaris and in 1575 there was a list kept of Anglesey gentlemen qualified to act as justices of the peace. Judges of assize would proceed from Caernarvon to Beaumaris with the supervision of the justices of the peace, as one of their ostensible duties. Serious doubts are cast on the efficiency of this supervision by a letter written by Owen Wynne to his father Sir John in 1625, advising him that the judge 'will not take gold from the justice of the peace but presents must be for the kitchen'; an instance perhaps of 'Tipping the Scales'.

The judge's lodgings are a house called Bryn Mel built, I would say, in about 1900, large and comfortable and with a quite spectacular view of the whole Snowdon range of mountains, often snow-capped, across the waters of the Menai Straits. Bryn Mel belongs to Miss Isla Johnston who has given it to the Church in Wales. It has a charming little chapel and the Church already use the house frequently for retreats and conferences. Twice I have had the good fortune to stay at Bryn Mel within reach of many friends.

As must be the case with a one-time member of Parliament, I think of the Parliamentary representations of the places the judges visit. For many years Anglesey was represented by a Liberal, Lady Megan Lloyd-George. She had no real time for the Tories and used to say of me that my only real claim to any sort of distinction was that I represented 'the gateway to the Principality', that is to say, Chester. Times changed, however, and there came a day when Lady Megan was defeated at the polls by a Labour candidate.

One day I travelled with Lady Megan from Chester to Euston and we shared a taxi from the station. Its course took us past the House of Commons and the light above Big Ben showed us that the legislators were in session. Lady Megan looked at the light and having been a Member for many years said:

'Whenever I pass the place these days, I say thank goodness I don't have to go in.'

To this I retorted:

'My dear Megan when you say that you have a gleam in your eye, and, what is more, it is the left eye.'

Within quite a short time Lady Megan was a Labour candidate for membership of the House and was elected soon after.

On my first visit to Beaumaris, there was very little work. This was often the case. On this first visit there was but one accused and he insisted upon pleading guilty. It was with the greatest difficulty that, between us, counsel and I managed to spin the case out for one hour so that there would be not too long an interval between the rising of the Court and the High Sheriff's luncheon which I think was enjoyed by my marshal James Curtis.

For the future the proposal is that in Beaumaris there should be magistrates courts only.

BRECON

The county of Brecknockshire must be one of the most beautiful in the Kingdom, with the Brecon Beacons rising to 3,000 fcct and the stark Black Mountains overlooking Monmouthshire and the river Usk winding through its wooded valley.

The assize and county town of Brecon stands where the Usk and the Honddu rivers meet. The town takes its name from Brychan, a chieftain of, oddly enough, Irish descent, who is said to have ruled hereabouts in the early part of the fifth century. Brycheiniog is Welsh for the land of Brychan.

In Brecon there are two places of special interest, the castle and the cathedral. The original castle is said to have been built by Bernard Newmarch in the late eleventh century, and when rebuilt was, I suppose, one of the chain of castles built by the English before Offa's Dyke. It was between Brecon and Builth that Llewelyn was killed in 1282 during Wales's second war of independence.

The cathedral became a cathedral as recently as 1923 when the Diocese of Swansea and Brecon was formed. Before that it was the Priory Church, built originally about the time of the castle, but rebuilt in its present form in the thirteenth and fourteenth centuries, a form which is rugged and full of strength.

During my visits to Brecon, I have always taken much pleasure in visiting the cathedral and the Dean has been good enough to arrange a cathedral service. There is an appeal to visitors to the cathedral to use this moving prayer:

> Lord, bless this cathedral
> That from it
> May go the truth that all men need to know,
> That in it
> May be offered a worship as fine as man can make
> That to it
> May come all who need thy help
> And coming, find it.

Brecon, in common with the other Welsh assize towns, became an assize town in the early part of the nineteenth century following the absorption into the English system of the Welsh Courts. The history of this should be shortly recalled. By a statute of Henry VIII, it was decreed that a Court of Great

The Courts, Brecon

Sessions, so described no doubt to distinguish it from the Quarter Sessions, should sit in every Welsh Shire, twice a year before one justice. In the reign of Queen Elizabeth I an additional judge was appointed to each Welsh circuit, the senior judge being designated Chief Justice. Wales was divided into four circuits: two for the north with Chester attached (the gateway to the Principality) and two for the south. The Brecknock Circuit consisted of the counties of Brecknock, Radnor and Glamorgan. The judges were appointed for life—and as is pointed out in connection with the assizes in Anglesey—some of the appointments cannot have been very satisfactory. In 1820 a Commission of Enquiry was set up consisting of Welsh Members of Parliament. In 1828 Earl Cawdor wrote to the Lord Chancellor pointing to 'glaring abuses'. A Royal Commission was then set up and under William IV, the old system was abolished, and in 1831 two English judges took the first assizes in Brecon.

A description of the first assize was published in *The Cambrian* for the 19 March 1831. It appears that an impressive concourse of personages set out after dining at the Castle Hotel and the Swan Inn to meet Mr Baron Bolland, the first judge to attend since the change in the system. It included the High Sheriff, the Chairman of County Quarter Sessions, the Recorder, the Archdeacon, and the Bailiff of Brecon and practically all the tradesmen of the town in numerous carriages or on horseback. At a point three miles away on the Carmarthen road, they met the judge and escorted him to Brecon where the Commission was opened in due form.

On the following Monday the judge addressed the Grand Jury expressing gratitude for the respect and welcome given to him and saying that it was the wish of the legislature that Wales should benefit from the new system. In these days of long, long lists it is interesting to notice that—I think I am right—only eight prisoners were before the Court and one civil case. It is also to be noticed that one man found guilty of breaking and entering and stealing was sentenced to death.

During my last visit I called upon the Bishop and Mrs Thomas to find, among other guests, Mrs Thomas's brother Dr R. L. James, Head Master of Harrow, a close friend. He told me that he had been addressing a women's meeting on some educational subject in Carmarthen. He had expected a handful in the audience and had found some 600. I have no doubt his speech was a great success although he would not admit it, and that it was prepared with care. As Lord Chief Justice Hewart (whose robes were ultimately handed down to me) used to say:

> An impromptu speech is seldom if ever worth the paper upon which it is written.

Save that the courts are Her Majesty's courts, the following is scarcely material. The Queen honoured Harrow with a visit during Quater Centenary celebrations and I remember then a passage from Dr James's words of welcome before 700 boys:

> We hope that whatever other impressions she (Her Majesty the Queen) may have formed of us during her visit to the school, she will feel that in this small corner of her realm, we are all her most loyal, devoted and grateful subjects.

It is the word 'grateful' which specially appeals to me.

For the future, the proposal is that in Brecon there should be magistrates' courts only.

CAERNARVON

Caernarvon, at the western end of the Menai Straits, owes its origin to Hugh Lupus, Earl of Chester, who fortified the place in 1098.

The Castle which belongs to the Crown was begun in 1283 by Edward I and completed by his son. It was twice unsuccessfully besieged by Owen Glyndwr. During the Civil War it was garrisoned for the King, but was captured by the forces of Parliament in 1646. It was ordered to be demolished in 1660, but, fortunately for posterity, the order was not carried out.

The Investiture of H.R.H. Prince Charles as Prince of Wales in 1969, the 21st Prince of the English line, has, through television and otherwise, made widely known the splendid dignity of this ancient fortress and the importance and attraction of this Royal Borough.

The assizes for the county of Caernarvonshire are held in the County Hall and have been since 1864 and the service preceding the opening of the assizes has been at St Mary's Church.

The Courts of Great Sessions in Wales—to which reference is made elsewhere—were abolished in 1830 and replaced by assize courts of the English circuit system. This change was strongly opposed by Welsh Members of Parliament.

The County Hall, Caernarvon

The first assize court in Caernarvon was held on 14 March 1831, when Sir Norman Tindal presided and expressed the hope that the new system would prove of benefit. In the course of his observations he said:

Another circumstance of a nature likely to prove highly beneficial to the public is that the errors of juries and those of judges (for judges like all other men are liable to error) will be open to the correction of the higher courts.

At the first assize to be held in the refurbished County Hall in 1864, there were apparently two prisoners for trial, one was imprisoned for three months for stealing a watch and chain; the other six months for stealing joiner's tools. This was the sort of size of calendar which enabled the judges of earlier days to see something of the beauty of Caernarvonshire. Times alas have greatly changed.

The present Under Sheriff of the county recalls how the court in 1942 was transferred to the judge's lodgings at Glen Benno. Mr Justice McNaghten, when walking on the evening of Commission Day, fell while trying to cross a stream. He sat next day but was in much pain. The High Sheriff, fortunately, was a doctor of medicine, Dr Griffith Evans: he examined the judge and diagnosed broken ribs and advised the judge to remain in bed. On the following day the Under Sheriff and the judge's clerk turned the dining room at the judge's lodgings into 'a passable court' and the rest of the business of the assize was completed there.

The judge's lodgings have for some time been a house called Plas Dinas, owned by another Oxford friend of mine, the late Mr Ronald Armstrong-Jones and his sister Lady Buckley, wife of Lord Justice Buckley. It is a charming Welsh manor-house with attractive walks to the sea.

Again, upon a personal note, I remember very well sharing a bell tent with Major Ronald Armstrong-Jones, as he then was, in the summer of 1944 waiting for the invasion of Europe; and we were encamped of all places on Wentworth Golf Course. I also remember bicycling over to Eton to see his son Anthony, now the Earl of Snowdon. His father, whose death was so greatly regretted, and I, had no illusions as to our part in the invasion. I embarked for Normandy to join another old friend, Colonel William Blackhurst, in my tank landing craft on D + 56; he was

Plas Dinas, near Caernarvon

Plas Dinas, near Caernarvon

n little bit later than that and we were armed in the main with the Manual of Military Law and King's Regulations. None the less it was all extremely interesting including the international crisis which was almost caused by the loss of Major Armstrong-Jones's bicycle somewhere in France.

In Caernarvon it is to be expected that the minds of those who remember him turn to the Right Honourable Gentleman, the Member for Caernarvon Boroughs, the great Prime Minister and leader in the First World War, Mr David Lloyd-George. I only just remember him in the House of Commons but I have known and had much regard for Lady Megan Lloyd-George, her brother Mr Gwilym Lloyd-George later Lord Tenby, and her sister Lady Olwen Carey Evans. It is not very long since I used to meet Mr Lloyd-George's brother Mr William George, a solicitor in Pwllelhi, who attended daily at his office until he was a hundred years old. In early days he and his son used to brief me, which I regarded as a distinction.

Of the great man, one of his admirers Lord Morris of Borth-y-Gest, a Lord of Appeal in Ordinary, a friend for many years and until recently Chairman of the Caernarvonshire Quarter Sessions tells this amusing story. Owen Williams was such a devotee of Mr Lloyd-George, who was then a young minister in the Government, that his admiration bordered on idolatry. With him one day on Ruabon Station was Goronway Parry, whose regard for Lloyd-George was only moderate. Both these persons I should add are fictitious.

'Look Goronwy, look man,' said Owen Williams in a great state of excitement. 'There he is the greatest statesman we have—there he is himself in the flesh and quite close to us. Make a note man and never forget this great moment in your life. It is a moment I shall for ever remember.'

'Well, well Owen,' said Goronwy, 'I hear what you say but after all Mr Lloyd-George is not God Almighty.'

'No, no,' said Owen. 'You are quite right, right indeed, but after all he is a young man yet.'

For the future the proposal is—and I think it will be strongly opposed by those devotedly associated with the Royal Borough —that in Caernarvon there should be a High Court and a Crown Court served by High Court and Circuit judges *until* courts are available at Bangor.

The Town Hall, Lampeter

LAMPETER

Very little information is available as to the history of the courts in Lampeter. The Lord Lieutenant of Cardiganshire tells me that he has papers and the pleadings in a case heard at the Great Sessions in Cardigan in 1669. It will be remembered that the Welsh system of Sessions ceased in the early part of the nineteenth century and was replaced by the English assize system. About this time the courts were held in Lampeter probably because of the opening of the railway and the building of the Town Hall and the Courthouse by a family of landowners —the Harfords—who were Bristol bankers.

I was very glad to be able to visit Lampeter where I knew a member of the staff of the University, and to meet and get to know Major Rhydian Llewellyn, then High Sheriff, and his wife. Sunday luncheon at their isolated house on the high hills some miles away was a delightful occasion.

At one of the functions in Lampeter I remember a discussion about some odd announcements appearing in the Press from time to time.

The Lodgings, Lampeter

One prominent paper reported in detail the local Conservative fête—the entertainments provided, the dresses worn by some of the important ladies and so on and then went on

> Then came the highlight of the evening when a telegram was read from the Member of Parliament regretting that he was unable to be present.

Another newspaper permitted itself to insert this advertisement for a local dance hall:

> Clean and decent dancing every night except Sunday.

There was very little work at the assizes.

The judges' lodgings were at the house of the Town Clerk let for the purpose.

For the future the proposal is that in Lampeter there should be magistrates' courts only.

CARMARTHEN

There is a record showing that there was a High Sheriff of Carmarthenshire in 1539 and it can be assumed that superior courts have been held in the county, at least, since that date. At one time, it was urged that the assizes should sit at Llanelli but this was strongly resisted by the people of Carmarthen. This is another instance of public opinion regarding a town as having added status if the assizes are held there.

The present court building, the Guildhall, has been used as the assize court since very early in the eighteenth century, but restoration has taken place and improvements have been made.

One of the interesting events in the history of the county is the Rebecca insurrection, which started in 1843. At this time, it appears, that there was, in this part of the Principality, a multiplicity of toll gates. There then arose a conspiracy, aimed at the destruction of these toll gates, so that the people might use the King's highway freely. Thus it was that some five or six hundred men, mostly mounted and armed with guns, hatchets, sledge hammers and pick axes, made their way, nightly, through the counties of Carmarthen, Pembroke, Cardigan and Brecon throwing down toll gates and committing other excesses. The raiding party was led by a tall man dressed, for some reason not disclosed, in women's clothing, and referred to as Rebecca. The

High Sheriff's luncheon party, Cardiganshire: The Rev. Roy Davies, Lady Honor Llewellyn, Timothy Barnes (marshal), The High Sheriff, Mrs and Mr Melvyn Evans (see p. 191)

The Guildhall, Carmarthen

magistrates sought to take strong measures against the insurrectionists with the aid of the Militia, but, in spite of this, the raids continued for several months.

Among recent Carmarthen cases of special moment should be mentioned that of a Polish farmer charged with murder in about 1954. The trial was sent over to Swansea but Mr Justice Oliver ordered that the High Sheriff of Carmarthenshire, in whose county the crime was said to have been committed, should sit with him. It may be that this is the only instance—or one of very few—when a High Sheriff has attended officially a trial outside his own county.

In the fastness of this county the vagaries of the weather have often been noteworthy. Mr Justice Havers presided some years ago at what is still remembered as the celebrated 'Lime' case. It began on 5 March and ended on 30 June. On the first day of the trial the judge had to walk from his lodgings to his car which, because of heavy snow, could not reach the door. On the last day of the trial, junior counsel celebrated the end of what was something of an endurance test, by taking a swim in the sea at Llanstephan.

In November 1931 the river Towy overflowed and made the

Brynderwen, Carmarthen

Cwmgwili, Carmarthen

main bridge unusable. The prisoners were, on this occasion, rowed across the river in boats.

On at least one other occasion such was the severity of a snow storm that no-one at all was able to make the journey to the assize court.

When I went to Carmarthen the judges' lodgings were at Brynderwen, an attractive house with lovely views of the countryside.

Since then the lodgings have been at Cwmgwili.

For the future the proposal is that at Carmarthen there should be a Crown Court served by High Court and Circuit judges.

CHESTER

My friend Canon Jarman has written:

> Nearly two thousand years have passed since the Roman Legion made a fortress on a low sandstone hill at the head of the estuary of the Dee and called the station Deva. It became the head-quarters of the 20th Roman Legion in Britain. But the Legion was withdrawn about AD 400 and the protection it had given to these parts ceased, the fortress was deserted for a long time and the Britons exposed to the incursions of Saxons and Scots. Ethelfrith the pagan King of Northumbria in AD 615 fought with the Welsh and the city was destroyed and lay in ruins. It was still derelict when in 894 a Danish army wintered here. In late Saxon times Chester gained in importance having its own mint (it had its own Assay Office until a few years ago) and a sturdy independence was emerging. After the Conquest Chester became a County Palatine and the seat of Government of the palatine earls. The Prince of Wales is Earl of Chester. Fortunes changed and Chester began 'to lose its standing as a port through the gradual silting up of the Dee estuary and the city was further impoverished by the in-roads of the Welsh'.

Chester has had its sheriffs since 1238 and, by the Great Charter of Henry VII, the city was constituted a county of itself. Chester's most distinctive architectural feature is the Rows.

> These are unique and justly world famous. They consist of a double tier of shops, one at ground level and the other at first floor level, each provided with a footway, the upper one being set back and covered by the second storeys of the buildings.

Their origin has never been satisfactorily explained.

In an old guide book of 1909, one reads of the Yacht Inn in Watergate Street where it is said that Dean Swift, annoyed that none of the Cathedral dignitaries responded to his invitation to sup with him, scratched on a window pane the following sharp couplet:

Rotten without and mouldering within
This place and its clergy are nearly akin.

Close to the Grosvenor Bridge over the Dee and within the county, is the castle, part of which dates from the time of William I. Some of the buildings are used as barracks and, of special note here, some for the courts of assize. The present buildings were built by Harrison shortly after 1797.

Up to 1542 business normally dealt with at assizes was dealt with in Cheshire at the County Court presided over by the Justice of Chester, and Chester was not therefore included in the circuit of judges of assize. In 1542 however the Act establishing Great Sessions in Wales included Chester; the County Court became the Court of Sessions and the Justice of Chester's jurisdiction, which already included Flintshire, was extended to Denbigh and Montgomery. The Courts of Sessions were abolished in 1830 and Chester was then assimilated into the national system of assize circuits.

Coming to more recent times javelin men ceased to be provided in about 1924 and a State Coach was last used in 1926. An interesting ceremony took place on 7 February 1930: the unveiling of oak panels containing the names of the High Sheriffs of the county from the year 1135. Lord Daresbury called upon Mr Justice Hawke and Mr Justice McNaghten to unveil the panels.

When the judges come to Chester, the senior judge takes command of the garrison and, having inquired as to the well-being of the troops, inspects the parade, including, of course, the band. It is also an old custom that the General Officer Commanding, Western Command, invites the judges to luncheon in the headquarters mess at the castle on the first day of the assize. This agreeable custom must, I suppose, cease when, as is expected, Chester is no longer the headquarters of Western Command.

The judges' lodgings have since 1948 been at Upton Heyes, an attractive house in Upton about two miles out of the city and

Inspecting the Parade at the Castle, Chester.
Nield, J., Veale, J., Col. David Bateson (High Sheriff)

Upton Heyes, near Chester

Dinner at the Town Hall, Chester.
Nield, J., Veale, J., Commander Critchley (marshal),
Lady Veale, the Mayor

almost surrounded by the Chester Zoo, to which the judges have a key very kindly provided by Mr Mottershead, the Curator.

Upton Heyes belonged to very old friends, Mr and Mrs Harry Beresford-Jones, and two of their grandsons have been my marshals.

Since my family lived at Upton for many years, (the house, Upton Grange, was pulled down in 1970, and now on the site is a road flatteringly called 'Nield Court') and since I represented the City of Chester, a County Division in the House of Commons from 1940 to 1956, I hope a rather personal approach to this part of the record will be forgiven.

I went to Chester as judge in Commission in 1961 with the late Mr Justice Veale and his wife and with Commander Leonard Critchley as my marshal. Colonel David Bateson was the High Sheriff and I was surrounded by friends. To add to the friendly and family atmosphere of the visit my twin sister was the Mayor of Chester that year, not very respectfully referred to by our friends as 'The Worshipful'. She had been Sheriff of the City in 1959 when, among her duties, so far as I could see, was personally

The Mayor with the G.O.C., Western Command leads the local Bar
to the Cathedral, the Town Clerk, Mr Gerald Burkinshaw, in front

to hang any Welshman found after midnight within the city walls. The Chester city sheriffs are proud of the fact that, whereas the first mayor is recorded as taking office in 1238, the first sheriff took office in 1121. As mayor, my sister gave a splendid banquet for the judges of assize at the Town Hall and it is believed that the senior judge had something to do with the choice of wines for that occasion.

At this assize too the mayor persuaded the members of the local Bar, for the first and perhaps the last time, to accompany her and the General Officer Commanding, then Lieutenant-General Sir Edward Howard-Vyse, to the assize service in the cathedral.

I have wondered what the answers of the mathematicians would be if I were to ask what the odds would be against another set of circumstances such as I have described coming about, that is to say, a situation where twin brother and sister are respectively judge in Commission and Mayor.

While presiding in the Crown Court at Chester, on this occasion and later occasions, my very earnest hope has been that I should not recognize any of my old constituents and perhaps one-time political supporters in the dock.

For the future the proposal is that in Chester there shall be a High Court and Crown Court served by High Court and Circuit judges—Chester and Mold to be administered jointly.

RUTHIN

The name Ruthin is believed to be derived from the Welsh RHUDD (red) and DIN or DINAS meaning city. It is said that there was a red castle on the same site as the present one, which was founded by Edward I.

In 1400 Owen Glyndwr and Lord de Grey of Ruthin disputed the ownership of a piece of common land called Croesau. The Bishop of St Asaph tried to mediate but without success and on 20 September 1400 the followers of Glyndwr raided Ruthin, plundered it and razed it to the ground, leaving only three buildings unscathed, Nantclwyd House, No. 2 Well Street and the castle itself. Of these three buildings, Nantclwyd House is of special significance. Dr Trevor Hughes, who most kindly gave me a copy of his book *Ruthin a Town with a Past*, when I last took the assize there in 1970, describes the house thus:

Nantclwyd House, Ruthin

The gabled portico, carvings, wainscotting, stained glass windows, armorial bearings and curious gallery all speak of the antiquity of this building and in fact it is probably Saxon.

In the sixteenth and seventeenth centuries the house was owned by the Goodman family. Gabriel Goodman was Dean of Westminster for practically the whole of the reign of Queen Elizabeth I and in 1574 he founded the famous Ruthin Grammar School. The claim seems to be justified, however, that there was a school there in the 1300s. After the church service on the day of the opening of the assizes, the head boy of the school approaches the judge, as he makes his way in procession to the gate, and hands him a letter in Latin which requests that the school be allowed an extra holiday. It is the custom to ask that the judge's reply shall be in Latin or in Welsh. Whether in Latin or in Welsh, the request is always granted.

Since the early fifteenth century, Nantclwyd House has been used as lodgings for the judge of assize. Dr Trevor Hughes writes that, in less enlightened days, the entrance to the assize courts was surrounded with stout railings as a precaution against an attack upon the court in the event of an unpopular verdict. The attack had not come by the time of the First World War and then the railings were used to aid munitions work. Similarly, a police constable was posted outside the judge's lodgings to protect the judge from assault.

I have always taken the view, although recent events make

The Courts, Ruthin

me less sure, that attacks upon a judge are very unlikely. In a
criminal case the convicted miscreant has usually a much
greater complaint against the witnesses for the Crown, or
indeed the jury whose verdict it is, than against the judge. Such
attacks upon judges have, however, taken place. Was it not
Judge Sir Edwin Burgess who, having presided at a Conscienti-
ous Objectors' Tribunal and disallowed a man's application for
exemption from service, came across the applicant face to face
on Central Station, Manchester, whereupon 'this man of peace'
took a pistol from his pocket and shot the judge and wounded
him, but not seriously?

When I was last in Ruthin, the need for protection seems
again to have arisen. It was thought that I might be trying some
Welsh Nationalists for an offence and so, in case of trouble, I
was provided with a large Alsatian dog which spent the night in
the lodgings with, I am glad to say, his police handler.

Contempt in the face of the Court must of course be dealt
with sternly from time to time. At one of the London courts
there sat Judge Wilfrid Clothier. One day, having given judgment against a woman litigant appearing in person, she rose
from her place just behind the solicitors' seats, opened her large
handbag, withdrew from it a dead cat and flung it—happily
with poor aim—at the judge.

The judge adjusted his spectacles, glanced at the disappointed
litigant and said:

'Madam, that is gross contempt of Court. If you do it
again you will be committed to prison.'

The comment conjured up a handbag filled with a limitless
supply of dead cats.

In this part of the Principality the Welsh language is commonly spoken and an English judge may often require an
interpreter.

Having been at the Liverpool Bar as a junior, I was frequently
briefed in the North Wales courts. At one time in this period the
County Court judge was Sir Thomas Artemus Jones. I digress to
recall that he was personally responsible for a leading case in the
field of libel and slander. Someone had written a book describing
the 'goings on' of a Mr Artemus Jones when spending illicit
week-ends at Ostend. The author thought that the name
Artemus Jones could not be that of any living person. He was
wrong indeed and had, in the end, to pay £1,000 damages to

Mr Artemus Jones whose reputation, he said, was damaged in the eyes of his friends.

Sir Thomas was an enthusiastic Welshman and insisted, quite rightly, on anyone wishing to do so, giving his evidence in Welsh. I have particularly in mind a case in which I appeared about a right of way over the Denbighshire moors. The first thing of value in the conduct of the case was that I learned that the Welsh for 'right of way' is 'RIGHTOWAY'. I had thirty witnesses, mostly oldest inhabitants, to say that, ever since they could remember, people had walked or taken their ponies unhindered over the track in question. However, of these thirty witnesses, unbelievable though it may seem, twenty-three were called Williams. All had to be identified; for example, Williams the chemist by the church, Williams over the river and up the hill, and so on. After I had called my fourteenth Mr Williams (this sounds like a famous joke made by Sir Alec Douglas-Home) and he had advanced my case considerably, I took my courage in both hands and said

'Diolch-Y-Fawr, Mr Williams', which all will at once realize means 'Thank you very much, Mr Williams', in Welsh. At this Sir Thomas beamed at me and said 'At last the English Bar is awaking to a sense of its responsibilities'.

Thereafter my path was the smoother.

To conclude this record of Ruthin, let me recall that in 1868 the railway came to Ruthin. Less than 100 years later, after the Commission under Dr Beeching, as he then was, its passage through the Vale of Clwyd ceased for ever. If Lord Beeching's Commission's present proposals come to fruition, Ruthin will have not only no railway but will have neither High Court nor Circuit judges visiting the town. I can only say how sorry many High Court judges will be that this should be so.

Not long after the publication of the Beeching Report, I met Lord Beeching at a luncheon in London and he said 'Are we still speaking?' This, I think, showed much understanding and good humour, and, of course, we *are* still speaking.

For the future the proposal is that in Ruthin there should be magistrates' courts only.

MOLD

Mold, on the river Alyn, is in the south-eastern corner of Flintshire at the foothills of the Welsh mountains. The parish church, of the early sixteenth century, is most beautiful and the assize service has been held there since 1830. Mold has always been the assize town in spite of the claims of the county town of Flint.

Before the English assize system was extended to the Principality in 1830 the Great Sessions sat at Mold. It appears that these courts were held twice a year, and, as in the case of Quarter Sessions, at either Mold, Flint or Holywell. The court accommodation at Mold attracted much adverse criticism. The building was described as a 'half timbered antiquated structure known as the Common Hall of Pleas'. One Pugh, a travelling artist in the early 1800s, called it—

> 'a barn-like crazy old building appearing better calculated to receive, on an emergency, a set of strolling players than for the solemnity of a Court of Justice.'

Judges complained of the inadequacies of the accommodation and the inconveniences of dispensing justice under a leaking roof. Thus, in 1830, it was decided to build a new County Hall and the *Chester Chronicle* of 8 July 1831 reported—

> The 'Town Barn' at Mold, which we have so often stigmatised as disgraceful to the County of Flint, will be abandoned to the mice and bats immediately after the ensuing Assizes and a handsome County Hall erected in its stead.

This step forward, no doubt, put an end to the efforts of the town of Flint to become the assize town. Those efforts had persisted for a long time. In 1668 there is a record that the inhabitants of Flint petitioned for the assizes to be held there, as was the practice before the usurpation—

> 'that being the chief town, and affording better accommodation, and how they have built a new Shirehall and a commodious house for the Judges'.

In the summer of 1966 I took the assizes at Mold and was housed in a small private hotel hired for the purpose. It was not entirely a temperance hotel since there was a bar in the main room, the shelves of the bar being lined with bottles and the steel grill in front carefully locked—I suppose against any invasion by the tenant or his household. On the opening day of the Sittings I remarked to the High Sheriff, Brigadier J. H. Stafford, that I doubted if an assize judge had ever before officially received a High Sheriff in an hotel bar.

The County Civic Centre, Mold

This was a very temporary arrangement for, by that time, the Flintshire County Council had prepared plans for a new County Civic Centre at Mold to include Law Courts and Judges' Lodgings. During my visit I inspected the site about three-quarters of a mile from the town as well as the drawings. Further than this, I made a speech from the Bench congratulating the County Council upon their enterprise and expressing gratitude for their recognition of the need for good modern court accommodation and for their consideration for the comfort of the assize judges when on circuit in Mold.

When it was announced that autumn that the Royal Commission was to be set up which would no doubt be recommending many changes, I could not but wonder if Mold would cease to be visited by judges of the High Court and so the County Council plans come to nothing and my remarks prove empty.

However, the scheme for the new Centre went ahead and on 2 October 1969 the new Law Courts were officially opened by the then Lord Chief Justice, Lord Parker of Waddington.

I am told that the four new courts are excellent in every way and I know that Lord and Lady Parker greatly enjoyed staying in the judges' lodgings which are a large flat on the third floor with a roof garden and splendid views of the surrounding countryside. It is believed that these are the first purpose-built courts to have judges' lodgings attached to them.

Since writing the above, I have spent a week in these lodgings and found them excellent in every way as are the courts. It was a very special visit since it coincided with the opening of part of the building by H.R.H. The Princess Anne to whom I was presented by the Lord Lieutenant and who showed a considerable interest in the work of the courts.

My marshal, Keith Walmsley, was much pleased to have a Royal occasion included during his short term of duty.

Flintshire's foresight has no doubt contributed to the fact that Lord Beeching's Commission proposes that Chester and Mold should be administered jointly and that in each town there should be a High Court and a Crown Court served by High Court and Circuit judges.

CARDIFF

Cardiff derives its name from Caer—a castle—on the Taff, and the castle has played a large part since it was built, in Norman times, in the history of the City.

It is only in recent years that Cardiff has become entitled to the designation 'Capital of Wales'. It was in 1949 that a petition was presented to the King, praying that the Principality might have—as it had not had before—a capital, and, that the capital should be Cardiff. This claim was strongly challenged from north and mid-Wales. Caernarvon with its long history—and a Royal Borough—not surprisingly put in a claim; so did Aberystwyth and Llandrindod Wells. In the end, that is to say on 20 December 1955, Cardiff's claim prevailed and the City was officially declared the capital.

For nearly 400 years before this, Cardiff had developed into a place of high importance. When the Act of Union in 1536 abolished the Marcher Lordships, one of them, Glamorgan, became a county as in England, and Cardiff was the centre of Government in that county—the courts too being held there, at that time, in the Castle.

The Castle belonged latterly to the family of the Marquess of

The Mansion House, Cardiff

Bute, who founded the docks in Cardiff and brought much prosperity to the town.

Until very recently, when a house was bought in Radyr near Llandaff for the purpose, the judges lodged, during the assizes, at the Mansion House, a large Edwardian house in rather dilapidated surroundings, built on a very unusual plan. There are two front doors, entertaining rooms on either side of a large hall and a very wide staircase with a wing leading to either side of the house. The story behind this strange design is this: the original owner had two unmarried daughters: they are said to have disagreed upon almost every subject and so their father, foreseeing upon his death violent discord between them, planned his fine house so that it could easily and quickly be divided down the middle into two quite separate dwellings—one for each daughter—so that a measure of harmony might obtain.

It was always hard upon the Lord Mayor of the day to have to leave his official house to make way for the assize judges, and equally it was hard upon the judges to feel that their visit caused inconvenience.

A favourite walk which my marshal, Anthony Hidden, and I took was through the Castle, and its park beyond, to Llandaff

The City Hall and Law Courts, Cardiff

and then to visit the Cathedral, with the sculptured figure of
Christ, Epstein's 'Majestas'. Llandaff is one of the earliest
bishoprics and the City the smallest in the Kingdom.

Cardiff's City Centre, built in 1904, is a most impressive
conception and, near to the City Hall in the same renaissance
style, are the Law Courts—they are very fine indeed.

During my first assize at Cardiff one of the other judges was
Mr Justice Scarman who has for some years presided over the
Law Commission, which is a body charged with recommending
reforms in the Law. He was at Cardiff trying for the main part
divorce cases and I remember asking him if he would try a
small civil case to relieve my list of civil actions. The case was,
in fact, an exceedingly difficult one, involving an entirely novel
point on Bills of Exchange. It lasted a long time and, eventually,
made its way to the Court of Appeal and the House of Lords,
where my brother Scarman's decision was unhesitatingly
upheld. The judge, quite correctly, charged me with obliquity
in landing him with this really troublesome assignment and
myself continuing to cope with the claims of workmen falling
off ladders and what are called 'Runners'—often the sort of
cases where some of the evidence would indicate that two motor

Lady Veale, Scarman, J., Veale, J., Anthony Hidden (marshal)

cars, each stationary on its own side of the road and blowing its horn, had come into violent collision.

It was in Cardiff that the marshal to one of the other judges—not Mr Justice Scarman—came to me in a turmoil saying that it was being said that his judge was going to sleep on the Bench. Thus I was charged with the task of telling the judge of this allegation. It was strongly denied—the judge however is said to have kept his eyes more widely open afterwards.

This episode made me think of a story I read, long ago, in Sir Squire Bancroft's autobiography. He wrote of the great Henry Irving returning from playing in a charity matinée in London, one summer afternoon, by train, to his house beyond Basingstoke. He fell asleep in his corner. The train stopped and the great man woke with a start. He looked out of the window at acres of small red roofs and little square gardens. He did not at once recognize the place and addressed a traveller opposite—

'Sir, can you tell me where we are?'

'Yes,' said the stranger, 'this is Woking.'

'Ah,' said Irving, leaning back again in his corner, 'if this be Woking, let me sleep again.'

The new proposal is that in Cardiff there should be a High Court and a Crown Court served by High Court and Circuit judges, and further that Cardiff shall be the administrative centre for the Wales and Chester Circuit.

SWANSEA

The name Swansea is said to derive from the Scandinavian raider Sweyn, and a township, rising at the mouth or 'Ey' of the river Tawe, might well come to be called Sweyn's Ey.

The earliest charter for Swansea was probably granted about 1165 by William de Newburgh, the third Norman Earl of Warwick. The original Charter was lost but a copy was found at the Public Record Office at the end of last century among the evidence amassed by the De Braose family to support their famous case against the Crown over the lordship of Gower. King Henry II took possession of the Gower and Swansea in 1184 and in 1203 King John granted these lands to William De Braose. The King repossessed the property in 1207 but, under the pressures which led up to Magna Carta, he restored them to the De Braose family.

The Law Courts, Swansea

As in most assize towns, Swansea boasts an ancient castle. It was founded in 1099 by Henry Beauchamp, Earl of Warwick, but, in 1260, it was attacked and burnt by Llewellyn, last Prince of North Wales.

The Lords Marchers administered justice through their own sheriffs until King Henry VIII brought Wales into the English system. The Lords Lieutenant of the thirteen counties in Wales directed the processes of higher justice from 1694 to 1715, by virtue of their office as Lords President of the Council of the Marches.

From 1815 the Corporation petitioned on several occasions for the holding of assizes in Swansea instead of the assizes always being held at Cardiff. These efforts met with success when the assizes were first held at Swansea on 26 February 1835. The Cambrian newspaper recorded:

> A cortège of about 2 gentlemens' carriages and a train of horsemen went to meet his Lordship at Wynchtree Bridge to escort his carriage into Town. The commission read, the Court adjourned until noon next day, the judge going to church at 10 the next day. His Lordship said he was highly pleased with the Court.

The courts are now contained in a fine new building and I recall, with admiration, the posse of Police carrying silver maces, forming the judges' escort.

The judges' lodgings are in the Mansion House, a Victorian house up the hill behind the town and with splendid views over the wide waters of Swansea Bay and westward to the Mumbles. The house was built in 1858 by one Evan Matthew Richards, a forbear of His Honour Norman Richards, Q.C., formerly Recorder of Swansea and now an Official Referee. I read that Mr E. M. Richards in about 1868 was elected Liberal Member of Parliament for the county of Cardigan. Such was the surprise at his victory in the then Tory stronghold, that he was always referred to afterwards as 'The accidental member for Cardigan'.

On my first assize in Swansea my fellow judges were Mr Justice Widgery, now Lord Chief Justice of England, and Mr Justice Ormrod whom I had met in Normandy during the War. Lady Widgery stayed with us for a time.

We all noticed, on the terrace of the lodgings, a pair of six-pounder guns and enquiries disclose that they were cast in brass

The Lodgings, Swansea
Ormrod, J., Robert Reid (marshal), Lady Widgery, Widgery, J.

at Woolwich in 1804. After the landing of a French force at Milford Haven in 1797, the people of South Wales had much in mind the expected invasion by Napoleon. In 1803 one William Jones, a local merchant trading with America, called a meeting of merchants and shipowners for the purpose of collecting money for the purchase of four six-pounders to be placed on the hills commanding the harbour and to be part of the arms of the local Sea Fencibles. The Lord Lieutenant of the County persuaded the Secretary of State for War to permit this. The guns were never fired and when in 1860 the War Office set up a battery on Mumbles Head the four six-pounders were taken into the care of the Corporation.

Both in Swansea and in Cardiff the members of the Wales and Chester Circuit very kindly invite the judges to dine with them in their Bar Mess. Whenever I have been a guest, as the evening has advanced, it has been the custom for the member to sing Welsh songs either as solos or more often in chorus.

For the future the proposal is that in Swansea there should be a High Court and a Crown Court served by High Court and Circuit judges.

DOLGELLAU

Dolgellau must be situated in one of the most beautiful, natural settings to be found anywhere. Fuller, the commentator, notices the place in his usual quaint way. He says that it possesses five peculiarities:

1. The walls thereof are three miles high;
2. Men go into it over the water;
3. Go out of it under the water;
4. The steeple thereof doth grow therein;
5. there are more ale-houses than houses.

He justifies the first assertion by reference to the mountains which surround the town; the second by pointing out that, on one side, there was a bridge over which all travellers must pass; and the third by informing us that, on the other side, they had to go under a wooden trough which conveyed water from a rock a mile distant to a mill; as for the fourth he says 'the bells hung in a yew tree' and, finally, he tells us that the tenements are divided into two or more tippling houses and even chimneyless barns are often used for the same purpose.

The Courthouse, Dolgellau

Some seek to translate the name Dolgellau as the Vale of the Hazel, a tree which flourishes hereabouts. It is situated on the river Wnion and at the foot of Cader Idris.

Perhaps the most interesting piece of ancient history here is the record that Owen Glyndwr assembled the last Welsh Parliament at Dolgellau in 1405. The site of the building is still known as Parliament House, but is now occupied as an iron-monger's shop. Glyndwr, it may be remembered, studied Law in London and was employed by Richard II before laying claim to the throne of Wales.

The original Shire Hall was built in 1606 in an attempt to secure a monopoly of the county's Quarter Sessions, shared at that time with Bala and Harlech. In 1759 there were complaints that the old building was in need of repair 'for all other His Majesty's Subjects that have business to attend there, to secure their lives from any danger or accident', and a new hall was erected in 1761 which still stands in Queen's Square and became known as the Siop Goch (Red Shop).

A third Shire Hall was erected on the townward side of the bridge in 1824 and is in use today. Great Sessions, as they were called before the Act of 1830, and later the assizes, were held at

The Lodgings, Bryn Adda, Dolgellau

A view from Bryn Adda, Dolgellau

Dolgellau and Bala alternately but after 1872 they were held only at Dolgellau. Quarter Sessions from the late seventeenth century have been held at Dolgellau and Bala alternately.

When I took the assize at Dolgellau there was no criminal business and the Under Sheriff, I was told, inquired of my clerk if the judge would like to be presented with white gloves in accordance with tradition. To this the answer was of course, 'Yes, most certainly'. It appears that the reason for the question then emerged: a pair of white gloves was not to be found in the whole of this county town. To this, however, there was one place which was an exception, namely the judge's lodging. So it was that I lent a pair of my own white gloves to the High Sheriff in order that he might solemnly present them to me to mark the absence of discovered crime in his county. I need hardly say that a handsome new pair was sent on to me after my departure for Caernarvon.

The judge's lodgings were, and I think still are, at Bryn Adda, a charming house on the hillside with beautiful views and owned by Mr J. E. Tudor who was High Sheriff in 1971.

To the east of Dolgellau, on the Machynlleth road at Caerynwch is the house of Baron Richards, who was born in 1752. He became Chief Justice of Chester, Baron of the Exchequer and ultimately Lord Chief Baron. The old house, Plas Hen, is probably one of the best preserved of the old baronial houses built in Elizabethan times.

For the future the proposal is that in Dolgellau there should be a Crown Court served by Circuit judges only.

WELSHPOOL

Welshpool lies in the broad valley of the Severn in beautiful country. Its official name was Pool, or Poole, but in 1835 an Act of Parliament provided that it should be known as Welchpool— no doubt to distinguish it from its namesake in Dorset. It is very much a border town, Offa's Dyke being only two miles away.

The town grew around a church. As early as the sixteenth century a Celtic monastery was established there. No signs of it remain, but St Mary's Church—often restored and rebuilt since the thirteenth century—attracts much affection in the townspeople and also provides the setting for the assize service.

Welshpool

The Castle was begun in 1100 by a Powysian Prince and has been lived in for over 500 years. The then Lord Powys left the great house to the National Trust in 1952.

The first sheriff of Montgomeryshire was, it seems, appointed in 1541 and there is a record of an assize being held in Welshpool in 1614. The assize was held in the old Town Hall, but in 1814 it was said to be unsafe; the present Town Hall where the assizes were held was built in 1873. In the meantime there are those who say that the assize court was held in the church.

It was pleasant to walk up the low hills nearby—my marshal, Keith Goddard, referring to such a stroll as 'the ascent by the South Col'.

During this century the assizes were held alternately at Welshpool and Newtown. At Newtown the sittings were held in the Public Hall, but between 1939 and 1947, in the Regent Cinema. Mr R. J. H. Cooke, the Under Sheriff, has shown me a calendar for 7 May 1947, showing Mr Justice Wilfred Lewis as sitting in the Regent Cinema. The Court was required to rise before the evening performance. I notice that the calendar contained only two cases.

The judges are fortunate here to have a very agreeable house just on the edge of the town for their lodgings. It was acquired by the County Council in 1959 and decorated and furnished under the guidance of Mrs Dugdale, a daughter of the late Sir John Bankes, L.J. and the grandmother of Lord Davies of Llandinam. In this she had the help of Lady Stable who was High Sheriff of Montgomeryshire in 1960. It is traditional that we lunch with her at her house on the journey from Welshpool to Dolgellau. Her husband, as I have elsewhere recalled, was a judge of the Queen's Bench Division for many years and a most popular figure. A countryman, he rarely sat in London and indeed, was always unwilling to come to the Capital. There was an occasion, however, when his presence there was absolutely essential. It used to be the custom for all the newly-appointed Queen's Counsel to be called within the Bar by all the courts sitting in the Strand. When this is done the presiding judge uses this form of words:

> 'Mr Smith, her Majesty having been pleased to appoint you one of her counsel learned in the law, you will take your seat within the Bar accordingly.'

Mr Smith then takes up his position in the centre of the front row of counsel's seats, bows to the court, then to right and left to other Queen's Counsel, then behind him to the junior Bar, and then again to the judge. He then sits down. The judge then asks:

> 'Mr Smith, do you move?'

Mr Smith rises again, bows and leaves the court.

In 1963 both of Mr Justice Stable's sons, Mr Philip Owen and Mr Owen Stable took silk and so, as I say, it was essential that their father should call them within the Bar. When he read out the phrase 'learned in the law' he obviously pretended that he thought he must have misread it: he very solemnly adjusted his spectacles, studied the card with an expression upon his face of incredulity—then read it out again still with an air of incredulity but also with solemnity. The Bar was delighted. This story can be told since both Sir Wintringham's sons are distinguished leaders of the Bar.

For the future the proposal is that in Welshpool there should be a Crown Court served by High Court and Circuit judges until courts are available at Newtown.

Haverfordwest

HAVERFORDWEST

As in the case of so many assize towns, Haverfordwest has a long history. It is claimed that it goes back to the fifth century, but it is sufficient to start with the twelfth. When the Normans moved west, the Welsh were driven from their native land into the north of the country, but the only way in which they could be held in check was to build a chain of castles right across Pembrokeshire. One of the most important was the fortress of Haverfordwest built by Gilbert de Clare, first Earl of Pembroke. about 1100 on an outcrop of rock overlooking the Cleddau river, In the early 1200s the walls were strengthened, running to six or twelve feet in thickness. After Cromwell captured Pembroke Castle, he ordered the demolition of the castle of Haverfordwest, but the building defied complete destruction.

Making one's way through the countryside near the town, it will be observed that some of the cottages are of unusual design. In 1105 the Flemings, driven from their own country by

St David's Cathedral

floods, were settled in Pembrokeshire by Henry I and their influence is still noticed. The Welsh language is little used and this unusual design of cottage has remained.

It is, of course, imperative that one should visit the smallest city in Britain, St David's, with its magnificent cathedral beside the sea. This historic city has a legendary place in Welsh history and it was said that two pilgrimages to St David's were equivalent to one journey to Rome.

The Royal Charter of 1479 incorporated the Borough of Haverfordwest and a mayor, sheriff, two bailiffs and burgesses were allowed; it also conferred the designation of the 'County of the Town of Haverfordwest'. A Statute of 1543 enacted that Haverfordwest should be a county in itself, separate from the county of Pembroke and with its own Great Sessions.

Thus, before the assizes ceased to be held in Haverfordwest which was in 1970, there were two Commissions and consequently two sheriffs. During the reading of the Commission at the assizes, held until the end in the Shire Hall, the County Sheriff stood on the judge's right and the Town Sheriff on his left.

It is interesting to notice that the immediate family of the present Under Sheriff, Mr H. P. Williams, held the office with a break of one year only for eighty-one years. Travelling round the different circuits, it is very noticeable that the Under Sheriffs or their forbears or others from their offices have served for many, many, years. It is open to the High Sheriff to choose his own Under Sheriff but he is wise indeed to choose the officer who has undertaken the duties for years and knows them well.

The first assize day for Pembrokeshire and Haverfordwest was 8 March 1831 and the first case in the list was a prosecution of the Shoemakers' Guild alleging an illegal monopoly. It was regarded as of such importance that the Attorney-General of the day conducted the prosecutions. The defendants were convicted.

A large number of private houses have been used for the judge's lodgings. I was lucky enough to stay in a charming house called Cressbrough, about five miles from Haverfordwest, owned by Lady Dunsany. I was also lucky enough to have time to see something of Pembrokeshire. It was specially agreeable to visit Lord Merthyr, Chairman of Quarter Sessions, an old Oxford friend, at Sandersfoot, particularly as his fifth son, Antony Lewis was at one time my marshal.

I found it also impressive that at the service before the assizes sat, various high-ranking officers of the three Services attended.

For the future the proposal is that in Haverfordwest there should be a Crown Court served by Circuit judges only.

PRESTEIGNE

Presteigne, the assize town for Radnorshire stands beside the River Lugg, one of the main tributaries of the Wye and is another place of charm in the Welsh border country.

The Rectory belonged to John Bradshaw, the president of the Court which condemned Charles I, and it is said that his brother built the Radnorshire Arms in High Street in 1616.

In the days of the Great and Quarter Sessions before the English assize system was extended to Wales, the court sat normally at Presteigne but sometimes at Knighton. In the sixteenth century Great Sessions sometimes sat at New Radnor. The Shire Hall, where the court sat, is on the site of the county gaol and the records show that grim conditions obtained there. It was probably because of this that there were so many escapes from the prison. In 1825 one reads that all the prisoners escaped, after locking the gaoler in a cell, and taking from him his pistols and cell keys. The prisoners, although armed, were all rounded up with the help of the inhabitants.

As is pointed out elsewhere the penalties imposed in earlier times seem to us now to be ferocious indeed. In particular the sentence of death was passed for offences which, at the present time, would be regarded as almost trivial. It is true that many of those condemned to death were reprieved—but a reprieve then meant transportation for life or for several years. Its exact significance is not altogether clear to me but I have read with interest in Mr W. H. Howse's book on Radnorshire that an epitaph was quoted in a *Hereford Journal* in 1788:

> Here lies Tom Smith and what is rare-ish
> He was born, bred and hanged in this Parish.

One shocking case is reported from Radnorshire in 1805. A girl of 17 was convicted of killing her newly born baby in circumstances which would incline most courts today to make a probation order. She was sentenced to death by Mr Justice Harding whose homily I have read with great distaste but which is too long to be fully quoted here. Coming to the sentence he said:

The Courts and Lodgings, Presteigne

I am now to pass upon you the awful sentence of your lawful and inevitable fate in this world. It is that you be taken from whence you came, and from thence to the place of execution the day after to-morrow. You are there to hang by the neck till you are dead. Your body is then to be dissected and anatomised. But your soul is not reached by these inflictions. It is in the hands of your God— may that fountain of love show mercy to it when it shall appear before Him at the Day of Judgement.

Nine years later Mr Justice Harding was taken ill at Presteigne and died near the place of the execution of this tragic girl.

It is said that Sir Samuel Romilly, whose wife came from Knill Court near Presteigne, when Solicitor-General, was much concerned by the number of death sentences and hangings. He died in 1818 and no doubt influenced the legislation of the 1820s which abolished the death sentence for a great number of offences.

It is also said that Radnorshire juries were reluctant to convict accused persons even in the teeth of strong evidence. The Shire Hall records relate that in 1834 a very surprising verdict of not guilty was returned and, that, after it, one of the jurors disclosed that five of their number were in favour of a conviction and seven against and that accordingly they had cast lots as to what their verdict should be. Each juror was fined £5 and a new trial was ordered.

I opened the Commission in Radnorshire in the summer of 1966. Many of us remember with gratitude the kindness of High Sheriffs there and of the Lord Lieutenant, Sir Michael Venables-Llewellyn, Bt., whose hospitality always included some excellent fishing for those who appreciated it.

For the future the proposal is that in Presteigne there should be magistrates' courts only.

CHAPTER X

Western Circuit

O N THE Western Circuit were the following towns:

Bodmin
Exeter
Dorchester
Bristol
Winchester
Taunton
Wells
Devizes
Salisbury

BODMIN

The name Bodmin means the 'Abode of the Monks' and the town appears to have been recognized as the county town because it included the largest monastery in the county. The mayoral chain of office has a notable badge depicting King Athlestan (A.D. 928) who granted lands to Bodmin Monastery.

It was the only Cornish town recorded in the Domesday Book.

The fifteenth-century parish church where the assize service has hitherto been held, is the largest in Cornwall and exceedingly impressive. It is dedicated to St Petroc, the great Celtic Saint, whose name is born by so many places of worship in the West Country and in Brittany.

Bodmin has not always been the assize town for the county of Cornwall. In ancient times the assizes were, almost invariably, held at Launceston and one reason advanced for this was that it was not safe for the judges to travel across the Bodmin Moor. They were held in Bodmin in the time of Henry III and Edward II, but later at Lostwithiel. However, upon a petition of the men of Launceston and the payment of a fine, the assizes were transferred back to Launceston.

The Courts, Mount Folly, Bodmin

In January 1664 the Cornish Members of Parliament petitioned the King, praying for the transfer of the assizes to Bodmin and stating that Bodmin had a public hall and all necessaries, while Launceston was at one end of a county eighty miles long, inconvenient to witnesses, jurors and suitors and improper in taking the deputy lieutenants and their officers so far away from some parts of a county exposed on two sides to the sea. At the same time there was a counter-petition from Launceston claiming to be entitled by Charter to have the assizes there. The problem was referred to the Attorney-General of the day, but was not settled for a considerable time.

In the year 1671 in the Bodmin town accounts appear several charges relating to the purchase of a mare to carry Mr Warden Kestell to London on the subject of the assizes. On 10 May 1671 is recorded:

> Paid to Mr John Wells for the town mare   £9
> To Warden Kestell to go to London   £5

The petition was not successful and the assizes remained at Launceston until 1715, when an Act of Parliament was passed providing that the assizes should be held in such place within

The Lodgings, Shire House, Bodmin

the county as the Lord High Chancellor, or Keeper of the Great Seal for the time being, with the advice of the justices of assize, might appoint.

Thereupon the judges nominated Bodmin as the place in which they designed to hold the ensuing assizes and the Town Clerk and justices of the peace were asked to make arrangements accordingly. In 1727 the assizes returned to Launceston. In 1836 an Act was obtained intituled 'An Act for Building new Courts of Assize at Bodmin in the County of Cornwall and for providing judge's lodgings.'

Priory Hall, where the court had sat, was taken down. This was unfortunate since it was a building of note, its roof being of the same design as that of Westminster Hall and having the largest single span of any hall in the country outside London. The church of Grey Friars was taken down and the new courts built on the site.

At the same time the present judge's lodgings, Shire House, were built across the street from the courts. The Shire Hall House is made extremely comfortable for the judges and, being in the centre of a holiday district, was quite often let to judges and their families for holidays in the summer.

Procession at Bodmin including Mr Charles Le Grice (High Sheriff),
The Mayor and Michael Sayers (marshal)

On my first visit my marshal, Mark Lennox-Boyd, took me to see his parents near Saltash.

Driving among the Cornish lanes is, as it seems to me, often hazardous and the desired route is not always easy to find. It is said of two Members of Parliament that, driving to inspect one of the china clay mines, they became hopelessly lost in the winding lanes. They came upon a kindly looking rustic and decided to ask for directions. The driver leaned out and said,

'Can you tell us, please, where we are?'

The rustic, who was not nearly so kindly as he looked, replied with a grin—

'In a motor car.'

The passenger Member of Parliament was about to explode with indignation but the driver leaned out again and said to the rustic:

'Sir, your reply is like the answer to a Parliamentary question; it is brief, it is true and it adds not one iota to the information already in our possession.'

When I last visited Bodmin, I was pleased to see again Truro's cathedral, built at the end of the last century. Before this Cornwall was part of the Diocese of Exeter. To Truro have been moved from Bodmin the County Council Offices. Truro is nearer to Cornish centres of population.

The judges, I think, will be sorry to lose Bodmin where they have always been warmly received by the High Sheriffs and Under Sheriffs as well as by the Mayor and civic dignitaries and where great trouble has been taken to present a colourful ceremonial.

For the future the proposal is that in Bodmin there should be a Crown Court served by High Court and Circuit judges *until* courts are available at Truro.

EXETER

'When the Normans took over England in 1066,' writes Mr W. G. Hoskins, 'they found at Exeter a city already some twelve hundred years old.' By the year 1000 there was a gild in Exeter and somewhere in the City a gild-hall already existed. When the Normans arrived, there was a Saxon gild-hall in the High Street. In 1499, in the High Street, the Gild Hall still awaited its porticoed Elizabethan front as it appears today: this

The Gild Hall, Exeter

The Lodgings, Larkbeare, Exeter

was built in 1593. It is said that this is one of the oldest courts of Law to be used as such in the Kingdom. Since the city of Exeter is also a county with its own sheriff, the assizes for the city are held in the Gild Hall, the judge being driven from the castle in a carriage and pair provided by the city.

At the Conquest, Exeter refused to acknowledge allegiance to the Conqueror and in 1068 the city was besieged by William's forces for eighteen days during which those forces tried to undermine the walls and attacked day after day without success. Eventually there was an honourable surrender, William swearing that he would not harm the city and that he would not increase its ancient tribute. The Normans, however, were to take no further risks and began to build the castle on the hill called Rougemont, at the top of what is now Castle Street, where the Gatehouse built in 1068 still stands. The castle withstood a siege in 1136 and records show that considerable sums were spent on further work upon the castle in 1170 and 1204. The assizes for the county have sat in the castle it is thought, since about 1250.

The judge's lodgings at Larkbeare, in the Topsham district,

After an Exeter Assize Service:
Charles James (marshal) John Smyth (marshal)
Lady Simon, Barry, J., Simon, P., the author, the author's sister

were part of the Devon County Council offices: they are now in my view the best and most comfortable judge's lodgings in England or Wales. A sale catalogue of 1875 refers to the lodgings as 'a capital stone-built mansion house with mullions and dressings of hewn stone, erected without any regard to cost'.

The reason for its acquisition for the judges appears from the Quarter Sessions Order Book which records that on 4 April 1876 the Judges' Lodgings' Committee reported that Plymouth was petitioning for recognition as the assize town for Devon and that it was imperative for better quarters to be found for the judges, who had expressed strong opinions as to the unsuitability of the lodgings then provided. By October 1876 the committee reported that the house had been bought.

At Exeter: Miss Beryl Nield, John Smyth (marshal) Lady Simon,
Barry, J., Simon, P.

On one occasion in Exeter counsel was addressing a judge who had been promoted from the County Court to the High Court. Counsel wished to recall a decision of the judge when he was in the County Court and said:

'That decision was, of course, before your Lordship's ascension.'

'Do not put it too high' said the judge.

It is interesting to know that, just under a hundred years ago, a Local Authority was keenly anxious to have what must have been regarded as the added status of being an assize town.

For the future the proposal is that in Exeter there should be a High Court and a Crown Court served by High Court and Circuit judges.

DORCHESTER

Dorchester claims 4,000 years of history. About A.D. 70 the Romans established a camp on the site where Dorchester now stands and Thomas Hardy wrote of the town:

> It announced old Rome in every street, alley and precinct. It looked Roman, bespoke the art of Rome and concealed the dead men of Rome. It was impossible to dig more than a foot or two deep about the town's fields and gardens without coming upon some tall soldier or other of the Empire who had lain in his silent, unobtrusive rest for the space of 1500 years.

The town has been recognized as the county town since the assizes began to be held there in early medieval times.

Two trials must be mentioned.

In 1685 the Bloody Assize was held in Dorchester, at which Judge Jeffreys presided, to try, or should one say deal with, the Monmouth rebels after the battle of Sedgmoor. Macaulay wrote:

> The court was hung, by order of the Chief Justice, with scarlet, and the innovation seemed to the multitude to indicate a bloody purpose. It was also rumoured that when the clergyman who preached the Assize sermon inforced the duty of mercy, the ferocious mouth of the judge was distorted by an ominous grin. More than 300 prisoners were tried; 292 received sentences of death. The whole number hanged in Dorchester amounted to 74. In fairness it must be observed that many of the accused men admitted being guilty of high treason.

Judge Jeffrey's
Lodgings

Dorchester

At the time of this Assize the judge lodged in a house in High West Street and it was for many years the local belief that his ghost haunted the house, stamping furiously to and fro.

In 1834 The Six Tolpuddle Martyrs were sentenced to seven years transportation for the 'crime' of forming in their village 'The Friendly Society of Agricultural Labourers', forerunners of the Trade Union Movement. Led by a local Methodist preacher, George Loveless, the farm workers joined forces to ask that their wages should be increased from 9/- to 10/- a week, the rate paid in other parts of the county. Instead, their wages were reduced to 8/-, and again to 7/-, to teach them a lesson. It was a time when the Government was in real fear of revolution and the judge in passing sentence said that he must make an example of George Loveless and his followers. The prisoners were shipped off to Botany Bay, but, after two years exile, were granted a free pardon in 1836, after ten workmen in Dorchester, assisted by their Member of Parliament Thomas Wakeley, had campaigned for their release.

Some evidence of the severity of sentences in early days is to

The Lodgings, Hyde Crook, near Dorchester

be seen on a plate affixed to Grey's Bridge across the Frome:

> Any person wilfully injuring any part of this county bridge will be
> guilty of felony and upon conviction liable to be transported for
> life.

The assizes have recently been held in the new County Hall,
Top o' Town, where the assizes, Quarter Sessions and magistrate's court are held in the Crown Court.

The judge's lodgings are at Hyde Crook a few miles out of
the town, a modern and very agreeable house with a splendid
view of the Downs and, in the distance, the obelisk erected as a
memorial to Thomas Hardy, who was born in 1845 and died in
1928 and won renown as a novelist and poet. There can be no
doubt that Dorchester was the setting for his 'Mayor of Caster-
bridge'.

In 1931 the statue of the great writer, at the top of the Grove
in Dorchester, was unveiled by a great friend of his Sir James
Barrie.

For the future the proposal is that in Dorchester there should
be a Crown Court served by High Court and Circuit judges.

BRISTOL

Part of Gloucestershire is on the Oxford Circuit and includes the city of Gloucester—part is on the Western Circuit and includes the city of Bristol. By a Charter of Edward III, Bristol was constituted a distinct county in itself and the assizes in Bristol are those of the city and not the county of Gloucestershire.

The history of Bristol hardly begins until the subjugation of Gloucestershire by the Conqueror in 1068. Early in 1069 three sons of Harold set sail from Ireland at the head of fifty-two ships in order to reconquer the Kingdom. The townspeople of Bristol repulsed this assault and the fleet was afterwards routed by Geoffrey Mowbray, Bishop of Coutance.

Henry III permitted the town to choose a mayor after the manner of London. Edward III allowed the establishment of a wool staple and the election by the mayor and sheriff of forty of the 'better and more honest' men of the town to be a Council.

The maritime enterprise of Bristol has been worthy of a place that 'seems to swim on the waters' and struck the eye of Pope, the poet, as having its streets full of ships. Perhaps one of the more memorable of the voyages that set forth from Bristol is that of Sebastian Cabot in 1497, who was the first Englishman to land in America and the earliest to discover that portion of the continent now called the United States. The notice in a local chronicle was as follows:

> This year 1497 on St John the Baptist's day, the land of America was found by the merchants of Bristol in a ship of Bristol called the *Matthew*, the which said ship departed from the port of Bristowe the 2nd May and came home again the 6th August following.

It is interesting that Bristol became the first city in the Kingdom to establish regular steam communications with the United States, the first voyage having been made by the 'Great Western' in 1838.

This recalls an occasion, years ago, when an overseas Law student wished to join the Northern Circuit and was, after Bar Mess in accordance with tradition, required to state his pretensions. He was first required to give his name in full. He did so saying:

'Christopher Columbus.'

'What did he say?' asked Sir Herbert Stephen, the Clerk of
Assize and son of Mr Justice Stephen.

He said,

'Christopher Columbus.'

Sir Herbert turned directly to the candidate and said—

'Well don't do it again',

which should, I think, give no offence to our American friends.

One of the most colourful aspects of the assize ceremonial in
Bristol is the use of the city's State coach in which the Right
Honourable (this is correct) the Lord Mayor escorts the judges
first to church and then to court. The coach, with its escort of
mounted police, makes a fine spectacle as it is driven through the
city.

The judges' lodgings on the edge of the Clifton Downs are a
large and handsome house adjoining the Mansion House.

While at Bristol, the late Mr Justice Barry (son of a Lord
Chancellor of Ireland), a most highly-regarded judge, completed fifteen years on the Bench—a period of time important
for the unmentionable purpose of pension. The cook designed
a cake for the occasion with fifteen candles upon it.

The late Mr Justice Barry after fifteen years a judge

The State Coach at Bristol

The State Coach at Bristol

Bristol at Church:
Richard Wainwright (marshal)
the author, Barry, J., John Smyth (marshal), A. Spary (clerk)

If the judge is fortunate enough to visit Bristol at the appropriate season, he may be invited to dine with the Merchant Venturers, whose hall is but a short distance from the judge's lodgings. This is a splendid occasion and one on which one meets many of the well-known figures in this proud city.

It may have been to Bristol, but I am doubtful of this, that the late Mr Justice Donovan (afterwards Lord Donovan) came fresh from the House of Commons. He came with Mr Justice Ormerod to whom reference is made elsewhere.

Sir Benjamin Ormerod is a very large man—I would say 6 feet 5 inches—and Sir Terence Donovan was about 5 feet 10 inches. Sir Terence in a speech at Bar Mess said:

'I have ceased to be an MP at Westminster and become a judge on circuit, but strange to say I still find myself "under the shadow of Big Ben".'

Sir Terence, too, it was who when elevated to higher judicial rank, acknowledged the congratulations of the Bar and, knowing the interest with which senior members of the Bar watch out for judicial vacancies, said:

'I am indeed grateful for your good wishes, I only hope I shall not outlive my welcome.'

Unhappily Lord Donovan died quite recently.

For the future, the proposal is that in Bristol there should be a High Court and a Crown Court served by High Court and Circuit judges.

WINCHESTER

Winchester was originally occupied by Belgic tribes and became, under the Romans, one of Britain's largest towns. The figure of Alfred the Great dominates the Broadway and is a reminder of his enlightened court and of the line of Saxon kings who held their Parliaments in Winchester. The Normans recognized the city's importance and the Conqueror built his royal palace there.

What must be one of the most beautiful buildings anywhere is the mediaeval cathedral dedicated to the Holy Trinity, St Peter, St Paul and St Swithin. It was begun in 1079 and enshrines the bones of many kings, including those of Canute, the Dane.

To the south of Westgate stands the important thirteenth-century castle hall. The hall is used as an assize court and the presiding judge sits beneath King Arthur's Round Table which hangs on the west wall. Several early Parliaments and some notable trials have been held in the hall, including that of Sir Walter Raleigh in 1603 when he was charged with treason and condemned to death.

Judge Jeffreys presided there in 1685. At this assize the venerable Alice Lisle was tried for harbouring rebels at the time of the Monmouth Rebellion. The judge, in effect, forced a verdict of guilt from the jury and sentenced the prisoner to be burnt alive that same afternoon. Public sympathy was aroused and the clergy of the cathedral remonstrated with the judge. In consequence the execution was stayed for seven days, but all that these humane people could obtain was that the prisoner should be beheaded and not burnt. This is, indeed, a shameful page in legal history.

In modern times, in the spring of 1940, a fraud case was tried here which lasted for six weeks, the court sitting on Easter

The Cathedral, Winchester

Saturday and Easter Monday. The Sheriff and Under Sheriff prevailed upon the Treasury to allow a payment to the jurors engaged in the case and this is believed to be the first time that this was done. At present, of course, the jury is regularly paid for loss of time and for expenses.

In 1970 in the summer, a special assize was held in the Isle of Wight, presided over by Mr Justice Bean, to try the Parkhurst prison riot case. This must have been the first time for many years that the Hampshire Assize sat elsewhere than in Winchester.

At the Castle new courts are nearing completion.

The judges' lodgings are at No. 4 The Close and it is a delightful house. Being within the precincts, the Great Gate is locked at 10 o'clock each evening. If the judge dines out, he must remember to take the gate key with him which is about a foot long and of great weight. It has been known for this to be forgotten and elaborate feats of 'climbing in' undertaken. Here, also, it is customary for the judges to entertain two boys from Winchester College, the Prefect of Hall and the Senior Common Prefect. It used to be, as is so often the case in academic circles, that the guests should be invited to breakfast. It was thought that luncheon would be more agreeable to everyone. On this

King Arthur's Round Table, Winchester

occasion, as elsewhere, a letter in Latin seeks for the boys an extra holiday. When this last happened, Mr Justice Bristow, a classic, composed a most erudite reply in Latin which he thought, correctly as it turned out, that the boys would never be able to translate.

Before leaving Winchester, as we have always done with much reluctance, I must notice among the tombstones quite near to the great west door of the cathedral, one of special interest. It is:

IN MEMORY OF
THOMAS THATCHER

a Grenadier of the North Reg. of Hants Militia who died of a violent Fever contracted by drinking Small Beer when hot the 12th day of May 1764. Aged 26 years.

> Here fleeps in peace a Hampshire Grenadier
> Who caught his death by drinking cold fmall Beer.
> Soldiers be wise from his untimely fall
> And when ye're hot drink Strong or none at all.

At the Winchester Lodgings:
Peter Newell (marshal) John Smyth (marshal)
Barry, J., Lady Karminski, Karminski, J. (now L.J.)

This memorial being decay'd was reſtor'd by the Officers of the Garriſon A.D. 1781.

> An honeſt soldier never is forgot
> whether he die by muſket or by Pot.

There is, of course, a wealth of humour to be found among epitaphs, but one which I have always treasured went something like this:

> Here lies the body of Captain John Robinson
> of the Punjabi Regiment of Infantry
> who was on the North West Frontier
> of India on the 11th June 1789
> accidentally shot by his batman
>
> Well done thou good and faithful servant.

For the future the proposal is that in Winchester there should be a High Court and a Crown Court served by High Court and Circuit judges.

TAUNTON

Taunton means 'The town on the Tone', a river which flows through the centre of the town. After the Norman Conquest a new castle was built and the keep remains. In early times the Bishops of Winchester were Lords of the Manor of Taunton and the town became the administrative and judicial centre for a wide area under their control.

In 1685 James, Duke of Monmouth, was welcomed by Taunton as 'King' and many fought for him at the battle of Sedgmoor. Subsequently, Judge Jeffreys held the Bloody Assize in the Great Hall of Taunton Castle. Of 509 rebels, 508 were condemned to death, the trial lasting two days. Swift justice is often to be commended. This was perhaps too swift and may not have been altogether justice. Many of the condemned were ransomed by their friends and families and others were reprieved and transported for life. It is said that Judge Jeffreys dined at Tudor House in Fore Street, the house of Sir William Portman, who later conveyed the Duke of Monmouth to London for his execution.

The Shire Hall was built in 1858 and the assizes have hitherto been held there and the judges are housed in the same building.

The Shire Hall, Taunton

In 1934 in the Shire Hall Visitors' Book Mr Justice MacKinnon wrote:

> In a prize competition for the vilest achievement of Victorian architecture this building would be an easy winner . . .
> Apart from aesthetics, I may say, after spending four laborious days in the Crown Court, that the arrangement of that apartment, and of its many wooden erections, is the most inconvenient I have ever seen. . . . I imagine the 'Gothic' architect of this pile had never seen a Court of Justice at its work. He ought to have done so—from the dock!

In Taunton recently it was specially pleasant to meet Sir Geoffrey Streatfeild, whose report is referred to elsewhere in this record, and his wife, and also the one-time Judge-Advocate-General Sir Oliver Barnett and his wife, who is the only woman mountaineer I think I have come across: she was just about to leave for the Himalayas.

On both my visits to Taunton I have enjoyed most generous hospitality but, again, some of the invitations have included a request for an after-dinner speech. To agree to this, for me detracts greatly from the pleasure of the evening. Some unconscionable people produce the invitation first and the request to speak after one's acceptance. As to this I have a technique: if the invitation comes without the request to speak I reply personally as follows:

I accept with pleasure your very kind invitation to dinner and I think it most considerate of you not to ask me to make a speech.

The speaker on one such occasion opened I thought attractively by saying:

It is now my task to speak and yours to listen: if, as is highly likely, you chance to finish first, pray do not hesitate to let me know.

For the future the proposal is that in Taunton there should be a Crown Court served by Circuit judges only.

WELLS

Mr R. D. Reid writing of the City of Wells, says:

A writer standing on the hills above Wells and looking down upon the plain at his feet said, 'In Jerusalem only was a wider influence born'.

The Kings of Wessex set up their Governments here and this part of the country was also the cradle for the Church.

It would seem that King Ina of the West Saxons decided to found a Church at Wells, so called from the springs below the Mendips.

Reginald, Bishop of Bath, started to build the cathedral at Wells about 1180. The monks of Bath elected as their next bishop, Jocelin, brother of Hugh of Lincoln, who was born in Wells. Much to the indignation of Bath, he at once returned to Wells and set up his bishop's seat there.

The bishop's palace is one of the oldest inhabited houses in England, with fortifications and a moat.

King John granted a Charter to Wells and this city has preserved its character largely because there has been no great increase in population for many years. In my opinion it is one of the most attractive of places.

There are reasons for thinking that Wells was an assize town from the earliest times, although not a regular meeting place until the eighteenth century. By the end of that century Taunton, Wells and Bridgwater were left as assize towns and Bridgwater in 1853 lost its status as such.

The Cathedral, Wells

The Courts, Wells

In the seventeenth century a market house and Guild Hall were built near to the Bishop's Eye, that is the gate to the palace. In this Guild Hall were held the assizes, including Judge Jeffrey's Bloody Assize in 1685, the prisoners being kept in the cathedral cloisters and St Cuthbert's Church.

The Town Hall in the Market Place was built in 1799 and restored in 1934. The courts were rebuilt in 1970. The judges occupied an unusual house only a few hundred yards from the cathedral.

Visiting so many cathedral towns and realizing that among the judges promotion is often, although not always, sought as time goes on, I remember a story told me by Mr Justice Austin Jones, himself the son of a parson in North Wales. A bishop was strongly tipped for promotion to a vacant archbishopric and the Press was anxious to know if he was likely to accept the office. A representative of the Press therefore called at the palace. The door was opened by the bishop's young daughter. The reporter said:

The Lodgings, Wells

'I am most anxious to know if your father contemplates accepting this great position if he has been asked to do so.'
The bishop's daughter replied:
'I am so sorry I cannot help very much. You see my father is in his study praying for guidance and my mother is upstairs packing.'
For the future the proposal is that in Wells there should be magistrates' courts only.

DEVIZES

Devizes claims that the country around the town was the earliest civilization in England. About 1080 Osmond, Bishop of Salisbury, built a castle at Devizes. It was destroyed and rebuilt in 1120 by Roger, Bishop of Salisbury, who was Chancellor and Treasurer to Henry I. Twenty years later, Henry of Huntingdon described it as 'A noble castle, of great strength and surpassing beauty, there is not a more magnificent fortress in Europe'. Bishop

The Courts, Devizes

Roger, it seemed, built the castle at a point where the three manors of Rowde, Cannings and Potterne approached a common point and, it has been suggested, that the name of the town is a corruption of the Latin Ad Divisas: at the boundaries.

The market place in the town is of great interest and in the centre is a cross, the gift of Lord Sidmouth, who as Henry Addington was Member of Parliament for Devizes, its Recorder, and for three years Prime Minister of England in Nelson's day. On one of the panels of the cross is recorded the tragic end of Ruth Pierce, a native of Potterne. It illustrates how retribution may be exacted by infinitely higher authority than that of the judges of assize. On 25 January 1753, Ruth Pierce, together with two other women, agreed to buy a sack of corn on the market place: each to pay a third share of the price. One of the women collected the shares and discovered that Ruth Pierce was deficient, so she asked her to pay up. Ruth Pierce protested that she had paid the whole of her share and

'wished she might drop dead if she had not'.

She repeated this wish when, to the consternation of the crowd, she suddenly fell down and expired, having the missing money concealed in her hand. The *Gloucester Journal* states that the verdict was one of accidental death, but, in truth, the verdict of the jury was

'From the visitation of the Great and Almighty God she was struck dead with a lie in her mouth. And no marks of violence appeared upon view of the body.'

This awful event recalls the case of the citizen who, for years, had defrauded the Inland Revenue and, became smitten with conscience, yet feared to disclose his wrong doings. He went therefore to an accountant for advice. The advice was excellent:

You must make a clean breast of everything, hide nothing and bring the £5,000 which you say you have wrongly hidden away, in notes from your cellar, where it now is, to my office and together we will go to the Inspector of Taxes and fully admit your fault.

Next day the miscreant attended at the accountant's office with a sack of notes. The accountant started to count the notes, 1,000, 2,000, 3,000, 4,000, 5,000, 6,000, 7,000, 8,000.

'But you told me you had hidden away £5,000 and here there is £8,000.'

'Good heavens,' said the miscreant, 'I've brought the wrong sack.'

Charles I granted to Devizes the right to have its own Recorder and Borough Quarter Sessions and County Quarter Sessions and the Petty Sessions were all held in the assize courts.

A private house has always been hired for judges' lodgings and, when I was there, it was an attractive house called Marden Manor some six miles from the town. I was able to entertain friends to dinner there, and, in this connection, it will be understood that, whereas the judge takes most of his wines with him, it is not possible to carry vintage port. Ever since I was appointed to the High Court I have given my guests a good wood port and called it 'the 08'. Quite a number of guests have tasted it with added reverence but most know that a 1908 has gone off badly long ago. However my joke was not intended to mislead and always ended in laughter. There is of course a lot of rather spurious mystique about being able to tell the nature and vintage of a wine. As someone once said:

'You can look closely at the colour, holding it up to the

light: you can smell it for nose and aroma: you can roll it round the tongue and even taste a little: but in the end there's nothing quite so helpful as a quick squint at the label.'

For the future the proposal is that in Devizes there should be a Crown Court served by Circuit judges only.

SALISBURY

The original site of Salisbury was, of course, Old Sarum and it is said to have been inhabited in the Iron Age. Thereafter, the Saxons came, then the Danes and the Normans and a castle was built. Later this castle became Royal property and difficulties arose between the Church and the King. Eventually these were overcome by the removal of the cathedral to New Sarum. It was founded in the thirteenth century and Henry III granted the city its first Charter.

The cathedral's foundation stones were laid in 1220 and this masterpiece of Gothic architecture completed in 1258. Among its many treasures, I suppose the greatest is the best preserved of the three originals of Magna Carter which King John signed at Runnymede on 15 June 1215 and which was brought to Old Sarum by William, Earl of Salisbury. It has remained in the present cathedral since 1225.

The earliest Pipe Roll in existence is that for the county of Wiltshire dated 1194.

The assizes have hitherto been held at the Guildhall in the Market Place which was built in 1795 and replaced the old Council House destroyed by fire in 1780. It was the city of Salisbury which suggested the 'Barchester of Trollope' and the 'Melchester of Hardy.' In recent years the judge's lodgings have been at Lake House, a beautiful house some six miles outside Salisbury in an attractive setting.

Reference is made elsewhere to the early custom of making presents to the judges on assize, a custom which might be regarded as perhaps corrupt. It had been the custom of the Dean and Chapter of Salisbury to present the judges on the Western Circuit with six sugar loaves. Sir Matthew Hale, indeed an upright judge, hearing that the Dean and Chapter might have some interest in one of the cases before him, at once instructed his servant to pay for the sugar loaves. At another time, a litigant gave Hale a buck in order to gain favour.

The Cathedral, Salisbury

Discovering who the donor was, Hale refused to continue with the trial until the venison had been paid for. The donor complained that no such objection had come from the Chief Baron and other judges when similar gifts had been made.

The records at Salisbury disclose a striking example of the severity of sentences in earlier times. At the spring assizes in 1827 Mr Justice Park said that, though the Calendar was a heavy one, he was happy to find that the cases were not of a very serious character. Nevertheless it is to be noted that he passed sentence of death on twenty-eight persons, one of whom had been found guilty of stealing half a crown.

It was at Salisbury that a considerable discussion took place as to the desirability of seeing that the juries trying criminal cases should include women. Hitherto—and this was considered by a committee presided over by Lord Morris of Borthy-y-Gest —the householder test has had the result that few women are called to serve as jurors. In my view it is almost always desirable that there should be women members of the jury. In the case, for example, of a little girl who is said to have been sexually assaulted, she should not have to face a jury box filled with men. Further in my mind there should always be at least two women, if any on the jury, to keep each other company.

Sometimes women are deliberately kept off the jury by the Defence who think that they will be too sympathetic towards the little girl and so antagonistic towards the accused. This can often be achieved, since either side is entitled to challenge up to seven jurors without giving any reasons and this may exhaust the number of women jurors available or chosen. For my part I would abolish this method of arranging a jury of all men—or all women for that matter. One of my brother judges, Mr Justice Thesiger, not long ago required that there should be an all women jury. This, I fear, I disagree with.

On the lighter side, I was judge-advocate at a War Crimes trial in Hamburg about 1947, when some twenty-two persons were tried for shooting our Air Force personnel who had had 'to bale out' near Frankfurt. The wives of senior British officers stationed in Hamburg were much interested in the case and attended the trial from time to time. I regret to say that they were not quite so impartial as one would have hoped and one of them sent me a cartoon which I hope will amuse men and women alike.

Lake House, near Salisbury

The drawing showed the interior of a jury room. In one corner are ten men arguing heatedly and waving their arms about in anger. In another corner are two women perfectly cool and composed and one woman is saying to the other:

'That's the worst of these silly men, they are so easily swayed by the evidence.'

For the future the proposal is that in Salisbury there should be magistrates' courts only.

CHAPTER XI

Conclusion

FOR JUST over 800 years, judges of the High Court, known in earlier times as Itinerent Justices or Justices in Eyre, have journeyed from the Capital to preside at the assizes in all the counties of England and Wales. In addition to the first object— to strive to do justice between man and man—the system has involved a considerable measure of traditional pageantry which I believe has been found to be impressive and to have pleased and interested a large section of the public. Now that this part of our legal history draws to a close, to give way to what is hoped will be a greater efficiency in the administration of justice, it is permissible to look back and to look forward.

For my part I am glad to have spent all my life in the Law so far, under the old system: and to have been able to visit all the sixty-one assize towns. It seems to me that, given normal times and circumstances, it has worked reasonably well. Unhappily, the present time presents special problems, in the main owing to the increase in criminal business to be undertaken by the courts. This undoubtedly justifies some change. For the future, none the less, there is, I think, no reason why some of the old traditions and customs should not remain. The judges—High Court judges and Circuit judges alike—will I trust continue to be surrounded with an air of some reverence, which is, as I have pointed out before, for the office and not its holder. There can still be the association with the Church. There can still be some degree of pomp and circumstance.

In saying farewell to the old system, I am sure that all the judges who go on circuit would agree that we owe a debt of very real gratitude to a great many people in the counties which we have visited. Lords Lieutenant have often befriended us. High Sheriffs everywhere have shown us much kindness and hospitality. In Lord Astor's book *The Office of High Sheriff* it is suggested that it is almost the duty of the High Sheriff to invite the judge of assize to dine with him during the assizes. I am bound to say that I have found this embarrassing. However, experience shows that the High Sheriffs appear, at any rate, to enjoy entertaining the judges in this way and certain it is that the judges take much pleasure in these occasions.

On the administrative side, all the Under Sheriffs look after the interests of the judges with assiduity, conducting them to and from the lodgings, to the correct places in church and in court; always ready to receive suggestions for greater comfort in the lodgings; providing a car when it is needed and helping in a hundred other ways. It is I think the Under Sheriff who will be most missed by the judges under the new arrangements.

In the court itself the advice of the clerks of assize and associates and their deputies is always valuable and no doubt this will continue to be given in the newly-named courts of the future. Shorthand-writers are helpful, too. I remember years ago prosecuting in a fraud case at Manchester. Counsel for the defence foolishly suggested to the jury that his client was acting like a public benefactor. He was interrupted by the Recorder who said: 'Public benefactor—sounds more like Jacob Factor to me—don't put that down, Mr Shorthand-writer'. I never knew, but strongly suspect, that the shorthand-writer faithfully recorded this strange intervention, including in particular, the last few words.

A word of thanks, too, to the court police officers, prison officers and ushers. It is not always understood how much the dignity of court proceedings depends upon the maintenance of proper and polite behaviour. Once it ceases to be traditional that advocates—and indeed everyone present—should treat the court with respect, I am sure a great part of the prestige attaching to the manner in which our proceedings are conducted will be lost.

When the new Crown Court is started, it will be faced with exactly the same problems which confront the present courts of criminal jurisdiction and, of those problems, the most difficult of all is sentencing. What I greatly hope is that Parliament will cease to try to do the sentencing for the court of trial and will leave the decision to the judge who has seen and heard everything there is to be seen and heard of the case before him.

Again the great aim of the judges must be, as it always has been, to be just and to reach a just conclusion. My fellow-judges of the High Court are formally called 'Mr Justice': it is a designation not easy to live up to. It is, perhaps, only surpassed by the lay magistrates, who are called 'Your Worship'; a mode of address which I would abolish at once.

It used to be said of Mr Justice Avory that, when it was found that he was to preside in the criminal court, the guilty quaked and the innocent rejoiced. Is this the test of a good criminal judge? It is, I think, a good one but not the final word. To condemn the guilty coldly and with no spark of compassion (I do not say that Mr Justice Avory did this, but he may have appeared to do so) cannot, in my opinion, be truly just. Many will remember, as I well do, the incident in recent political history when a Minister of the Crown in a speech in the House of Commons falsely denied a failing in his private affairs. At that moment in his life he had lost, it might have seemed, everything: yet before that moment he had served his country and society with honour and distinction. Some compassion might then be said to be just. I recall a letter to *The Times* about this time, which included this passage:

> When sin and failing are weighed in the scales of human justice, it is only right that each who sits in judgment shall take the man's life as a whole into account before passing sentence.

Those of us who have spent a life-time in the courts tend to forget that others who come there have not. Jurors, I am certain, are bewildered by the strangeness of their surroundings and awed by the weighty responsibility of their task; witnesses are often bound to be nervous and, in consequence, somewhat halting or incoherent in giving their evidence; the accused, above all, is in an unenviable position, behind bars, between warders and often referred to as 'the prisoner'. Some human understanding and sympathy must, I believe, come from the Bench for all of these people. I remember once on a hot summer day in court a burly policeman in the witness box asking to be allowed to sit down as he felt he was about to faint. He was fearfully embarrassed but I think it helped him to be told:

> 'Do not worry, officer. This sort of thing happens regularly in the Brigade of Guards.'

Some years ago, a much loved fellow-Bencher of the Inner Temple, Sir Alfred Bucknill, a Lord Justice of Appeal, advised me to read a short life of Lord Birkenhead by a great Scottish judge, Lord Macmillan, and this passage in particular which I quote, because it has guided me and, I am sure, guides other judicial persons—

> Few minds are as neutral as a sheet of plate glass and indeed a mind of that quality may actually fail in judicial efficiency, for the warmer tints of imagination and sympathy are needed to temper the cold light of reason, if human justice is to be done.

This record began with the words of the judge's clerk when opening the assize in any county. In gratitude for the past and with cautious hopes for the future—for there are dangers ahead —I end this record with the words of the judge's clerk when closing the assizes in any of the sixty-one assize towns:

'All persons having anything further to do before My Lords the Queen's Justices of Assize may now depart hence and give their attendance forthwith at My Lord's lodgings.

GOD SAVE THE QUEEN AND MY LORDS THE QUEEN'S JUSTICES.'

Index of Names

Page references in italic type indicate illustrations

General Index

Page references in italic type refer to illustrations.